Published in 2020 by JCRM Publishing, UK

Designed and Produced by Ralph & Claire Moody

Copyright © JCRM Publishing 2020

ISBN: 979-8553372941

Advanced Coaching Journal : Reflection On Your Use Of Tools & Techniques In Coaching

Available from Amazon and other leading retail outlets.

If you would like us to create a bespoke journal for your organisation or work role contact us on +44 0800 302 9344.

If you enjoyed this journal please leave us a review on Amazon. Thank you.

www.jcrm.shop

Retail enquiries to:
info@targettrg.co.uk

Advanced Coaching Journal

Reflection On Your Use Of Tools & Techniques In Coaching

CLAIRE & RALPH MOODY

JCRM Publishing

www.jcrm.shop

In case of loss please return to:

....

....

....

www.jcrm.shop

A PERSONAL GROWTH GUIDE FOR YOU TO USE AND GROW

DEVELOPING COURAGE

Understanding confidence for personal improvement and long-term growth

By Claire & Ralph Moody

Your Free Book Is Waiting

Many people struggle with low confidence and low self-esteem, which affects their professional and personal lives. Your thoughts and feelings have a significant impact and this is where issues can manifest. If we don't do something about it, a lack of confidence will hold you back. This book will give you an opportunity to think about your confidence in a different way.

Get your free copy:

www.jcrm.shop

The authors also own Target Training and the company is recognised as a 5 Star provider by Trustpilot and our testimonials are legendary.

We offer training and coaching services and specialise in Coaching, Training, Management and Personal Development and all our courses can be delivered remotely online.

A sample of our courses include:

- Managing Staff Remotely
- Positive Mental Attitude P.M.A.
- Self-Esteem
- Train the Trainer
- Confidence
- Coaching Skills
- Management Skills
- Leadership Skills
- Mental Health First Aid
- Interview Preparation

Contact us at info@targettrg.co.uk

Our customers love us!

www.targettrg.co.uk or www.targettrg.com

ADVANCED COACHING JOURNAL

REFLECTION ON YOUR USE OF TOOLS & TECHNIQUES IN COACHING

A journal for you to use and grow

If you want a significant understanding of your coaching, then reflection from your coaching sessions is critical for your understanding of coaching practice. Many coaches get stuck and follow the same tools and techniques, adopting a tick box approach. If we are not careful, we will not develop our coaching skills further, and we will become stale in our practice. All coaches require Continued Professional Development (CPD) and effective supervision to maintain high standards. Sometimes coaches forget that using tools and techniques is their choice but maybe it's not the right choice for the client.

Our journals are designed to help individuals in any specific area they would like to change in their lives, both professionally and personally. We use coaching questions to guide your thinking in a different way.

A journal is perfect to write your reflections every day. All you need to do is write for five minutes at the beginning or end of every day or both if you choose. Writing in a journal can create significant changes in your life when done correctly. We have both benefitted when writing a journal as do millions of others. It's an excellent opportunity to create a habit and build this into your life and as an example, make it part of your daily routine.

The purpose of this journal is to encourage you to reflect on how much you rely on tools and techniques. it's an opportunity to really understand yourself to achieve your goals and success. Our journals are different they look at your thinking around the moments of decision making. It is getting to the route of the problem that creates the change looking past the specifics. We have written specific questions for you to use as a guide; these will help you in particular areas. If you sit with just thinking you will not notice as much as if you write. We felt a 100-day journal to begin with where you put all your reflections together would keep things simple for you. If you force yourself to write every day with your thoughts, you will grow in so many ways. You will be so much more successful in your life if you do this properly. Our aim with this journal is to encourage you to grow and focus to create change. A journal is perfect to record this; keeping all your thoughts and feelings in one place, incredibly powerful and very special.

Try not to make it a tick box exercise, so it becomes a chore. Make it something you look forward to doing, writing your thoughts and feelings on paper so you can reflect and look back. Create the habit and then watch how you develop and grow. The journal includes a page for every day for you to make notes, then separate reflection sheets for every 10 days and then the final page. Reflection is so critical when writing your journal to see what words keep jumping out.

If you find yourself writing the same things recognise this, then think why am I doing this, what change would I like? Then you can reflect on this and what you can do differently. This will help you think in different ways and what you would like to be different, giving you a focus. Think about how you think and feel, you want to notice differences in yourself to create change, change will be happening if you pay attention.

Forcing yourself to write in a journal will create much more awareness about how you can develop yourself, your mindset and your patterns. There is no doubt you will find yourself growing in confidence and becoming more positive about improving reflecting on your coaching skills. It is little changes that move you to create bigger changes, you have to be committed though.

Writing a journal is an amazing journey, good luck and enjoy the very special thoughts and moments as you watch a much more positive mindset taking place.

Ralph & Claire

Ralph & Claire Moody
Founders of JCRM Publishing

HOW TO USE THE JOURNAL

The session sheets are for you to complete each day. Make sure you complete all questions.

Every 10 days complete a review of your actions and reflect on what you have achieved. There is space on the right side for you to make notes along with some words of wisdom.

Before we start the journal some pre questions:

ON A SCALE OF 1-10 HOW MUCH DO YOU RELY ON USING TOOLS AND TECHNIQUES IN YOUR SESSIONS?

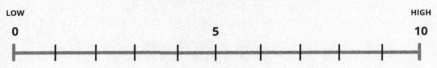

LOW

HIGH

0

5

10

WRITE BELOW HOW MUCH YOU USE COACHING TOOLS IN A SESSION. LOOK AT PSYCHOMETRICS, LEARNING STYLES, MANAGEMENT AND LEADERSHIP STYLES.

DATE:-   /   /

1: HOW MUCH GUIDING VS TELLING DID YOU DO? WHO WAS THIS FOR YOU OR THE CLIENT? WHAT COULD YOU DO DIFFERENTLY TO GROW?

2: WHAT MODELS HAVE YOU USED TODAY? BEHAVIOURAL MODELS OR NOTICING EMOTIONS AND FEELINGS? WHAT COULD YOU THINK ABOUT DIFFERENTLY FOR THE NEXT SESSION?

3: HOW MUCH OF YOUR WORK IS A HABIT? WHAT NEW HABITS WOULD YOU LIKE TO CREATE AND WHAT ONES WOULD YOU LIKE TO DELETE LIKE AN APP ON YOUR PHONE. THINK ABOUT ONE FOR YOUR NEXT SESSION.

4: HOW WAS YOUR CLIENT RELATIONSHIP TODAY, WHY WAS THIS? WHAT WOULD YOU LIKE TO BE DIFFERENT?

5: WHAT TOOLS HAVE YOU USED TODAY, WHY? DID YOU PREPARE TO USE THEM? IF THIS IS THE CASE WHAT MIGHT YOU HAVE MISSED BY NOT PAYING ATTENTION? WHAT COULD YOU DO DIFFERENTLY NEXT TIME?

6: WHAT WAS YOUR STYLE TODAY? AUTOCRATIC (BOSSY AND AUTHORITIVE) DEMOCRATIC (GUIDE AND PERSONNEL), LAISSEZ-FAIRE (MINDFUL AND RELAXED). REFLECT ON THIS AND WATCH HOW YOU CHANGE, WHAT TRIGGERS YOUR STYLE?

7: HOW MUCH ACTIVE LISTENING DID YOU DO? DID YOU LISTEN TO UNDERSTAND OR LISTEN TO REPLY? A KEY ERROR IS A COACH FORMULATING THE NEXT QUESTION INSTEAD OF LISTENING.

8: IF YOU USED NO TOOLS OR TECHNIQUES TODAY HOW DID THAT MAKE YOU FEEL? DID YOU LEAVE THINKING YOU MISSED SOMETHING? WHAT COULD YOU CHANGE FOR NEXT TIME?

9: WHAT PERCENTAGE OF THE SESSION WAS DRIVEN BY YOU? HOW MUCH OF THE SESSION WERE YOU RELAXED AND NOTICED WHAT CAME UP IN THE SESSION?

10: HOW MUCH OF THE SESSION WAS ABOUT YOU AND HOW MUCH ABOUT THE CLIENT? HOW COULD YOU LOOK AT THIS IN MORE DETAIL?

REFLECTION ON YOUR USE OF TOOLS AND
TECHNIQUES IN COACHING

DATE:-   /   /

1: HOW MUCH GUIDING VS TELLING DID YOU DO? WHO WAS THIS
FOR YOU OR THE CLIENT? WHAT COULD YOU DO DIFFERENTLY TO GROW?

2: WHAT MODELS HAVE YOU USED TODAY? BEHAVIOURAL MODELS OR
NOTICING EMOTIONS AND FEELINGS? WHAT COULD YOU THINK ABOUT
DIFFERENTLY FOR THE NEXT SESSION?

3: HOW MUCH OF YOUR WORK IS A HABIT? WHAT NEW HABITS WOULD
YOU LIKE TO CREATE AND WHAT ONES WOULD YOU LIKE TO DELETE LIKE
AN APP ON YOUR PHONE. THINK ABOUT ONE FOR YOUR NEXT SESSION.

4: HOW WAS YOUR CLIENT RELATIONSHIP TODAY, WHY WAS THIS?
WHAT WOULD YOU LIKE TO BE DIFFERENT?

5: WHAT TOOLS HAVE YOU USED TODAY, WHY? DID YOU PREPARE TO
USE THEM? IF THIS IS THE CASE WHAT MIGHT YOU HAVE MISSED BY NOT
PAYING ATTENTION? WHAT COULD YOU DO DIFFERENTLY NEXT TIME?

6: WHAT WAS YOUR STYLE TODAY? AUTOCRATIC (BOSSY AND AUTHORITIVE) DEMOCRATIC (GUIDE AND PERSONNEL), LAISSEZ-FAIRE (MINDFUL AND RELAXED). REFLECT ON THIS AND WATCH HOW YOU CHANGE, WHAT TRIGGERS YOUR STYLE?

7: HOW MUCH ACTIVE LISTENING DID YOU DO? DID YOU LISTEN TO UNDERSTAND OR LISTEN TO REPLY? A KEY ERROR IS A COACH FORMULATING THE NEXT QUESTION INSTEAD OF LISTENING.

8: IF YOU USED NO TOOLS OR TECHNIQUES TODAY HOW DID THAT MAKE YOU FEEL? DID YOU LEAVE THINKING YOU MISSED SOMETHING? WHAT COULD YOU CHANGE FOR NEXT TIME?

9: WHAT PERCENTAGE OF THE SESSION WAS DRIVEN BY YOU? HOW MUCH OF THE SESSION WERE YOU RELAXED AND NOTICED WHAT CAME UP IN THE SESSION?

10: HOW MUCH OF THE SESSION WAS ABOUT YOU AND HOW MUCH ABOUT THE CLIENT? HOW COULD YOU LOOK AT THIS IN MORE DETAIL?

DATE:-   /   /

1: HOW MUCH GUIDING VS TELLING DID YOU DO? WHO WAS THIS FOR YOU OR THE CLIENT? WHAT COULD YOU DO DIFFERENTLY TO GROW?

2: WHAT MODELS HAVE YOU USED TODAY? BEHAVIOURAL MODELS OR NOTICING EMOTIONS AND FEELINGS? WHAT COULD YOU THINK ABOUT DIFFERENTLY FOR THE NEXT SESSION?

3: HOW MUCH OF YOUR WORK IS A HABIT? WHAT NEW HABITS WOULD YOU LIKE TO CREATE AND WHAT ONES WOULD YOU LIKE TO DELETE LIKE AN APP ON YOUR PHONE. THINK ABOUT ONE FOR YOUR NEXT SESSION.

4: HOW WAS YOUR CLIENT RELATIONSHIP TODAY, WHY WAS THIS? WHAT WOULD YOU LIKE TO BE DIFFERENT?

5: WHAT TOOLS HAVE YOU USED TODAY, WHY? DID YOU PREPARE TO USE THEM? IF THIS IS THE CASE WHAT MIGHT YOU HAVE MISSED BY NOT PAYING ATTENTION? WHAT COULD YOU DO DIFFERENTLY NEXT TIME?

6: WHAT WAS YOUR STYLE TODAY? AUTOCRATIC (BOSSY AND AUTHORITIVE) DEMOCRATIC (GUIDE AND PERSONNEL), LAISSEZ-FAIRE (MINDFUL AND RELAXED). REFLECT ON THIS AND WATCH HOW YOU CHANGE, WHAT TRIGGERS YOUR STYLE?

7: HOW MUCH ACTIVE LISTENING DID YOU DO? DID YOU LISTEN TO UNDERSTAND OR LISTEN TO REPLY? A KEY ERROR IS A COACH FORMULATING THE NEXT QUESTION INSTEAD OF LISTENING.

8: IF YOU USED NO TOOLS OR TECHNIQUES TODAY HOW DID THAT MAKE YOU FEEL? DID YOU LEAVE THINKING YOU MISSED SOMETHING? WHAT COULD YOU CHANGE FOR NEXT TIME?

9: WHAT PERCENTAGE OF THE SESSION WAS DRIVEN BY YOU? HOW MUCH OF THE SESSION WERE YOU RELAXED AND NOTICED WHAT CAME UP IN THE SESSION?

10: HOW MUCH OF THE SESSION WAS ABOUT YOU AND HOW MUCH ABOUT THE CLIENT? HOW COULD YOU LOOK AT THIS IN MORE DETAIL?

DATE:-   /   /

1: HOW MUCH GUIDING VS TELLING DID YOU DO? WHO WAS THIS FOR YOU OR THE CLIENT? WHAT COULD YOU DO DIFFERENTLY TO GROW?

2: WHAT MODELS HAVE YOU USED TODAY? BEHAVIOURAL MODELS OR NOTICING EMOTIONS AND FEELINGS? WHAT COULD YOU THINK ABOUT DIFFERENTLY FOR THE NEXT SESSION?

3: HOW MUCH OF YOUR WORK IS A HABIT? WHAT NEW HABITS WOULD YOU LIKE TO CREATE AND WHAT ONES WOULD YOU LIKE TO DELETE LIKE AN APP ON YOUR PHONE. THINK ABOUT ONE FOR YOUR NEXT SESSION.

4: HOW WAS YOUR CLIENT RELATIONSHIP TODAY, WHY WAS THIS? WHAT WOULD YOU LIKE TO BE DIFFERENT?

5: WHAT TOOLS HAVE YOU USED TODAY, WHY? DID YOU PREPARE TO USE THEM? IF THIS IS THE CASE WHAT MIGHT YOU HAVE MISSED BY NOT PAYING ATTENTION? WHAT COULD YOU DO DIFFERENTLY NEXT TIME?

6: WHAT WAS YOUR STYLE TODAY? AUTOCRATIC (BOSSY AND AUTHORITIVE) DEMOCRATIC (GUIDE AND PERSONNEL), LAISSEZ-FAIRE (MINDFUL AND RELAXED). REFLECT ON THIS AND WATCH HOW YOU CHANGE, WHAT TRIGGERS YOUR STYLE?

7: HOW MUCH ACTIVE LISTENING DID YOU DO? DID YOU LISTEN TO UNDERSTAND OR LISTEN TO REPLY? A KEY ERROR IS A COACH FORMULATING THE NEXT QUESTION INSTEAD OF LISTENING.

8: IF YOU USED NO TOOLS OR TECHNIQUES TODAY HOW DID THAT MAKE YOU FEEL? DID YOU LEAVE THINKING YOU MISSED SOMETHING? WHAT COULD YOU CHANGE FOR NEXT TIME?

9: WHAT PERCENTAGE OF THE SESSION WAS DRIVEN BY YOU? HOW MUCH OF THE SESSION WERE YOU RELAXED AND NOTICED WHAT CAME UP IN THE SESSION?

10: HOW MUCH OF THE SESSION WAS ABOUT YOU AND HOW MUCH ABOUT THE CLIENT? HOW COULD YOU LOOK AT THIS IN MORE DETAIL?

DATE:-   /   /

1: HOW MUCH GUIDING VS TELLING DID YOU DO? WHO WAS THIS FOR YOU OR THE CLIENT? WHAT COULD YOU DO DIFFERENTLY TO GROW?

2: WHAT MODELS HAVE YOU USED TODAY? BEHAVIOURAL MODELS OR NOTICING EMOTIONS AND FEELINGS? WHAT COULD YOU THINK ABOUT DIFFERENTLY FOR THE NEXT SESSION?

3: HOW MUCH OF YOUR WORK IS A HABIT? WHAT NEW HABITS WOULD YOU LIKE TO CREATE AND WHAT ONES WOULD YOU LIKE TO DELETE LIKE AN APP ON YOUR PHONE. THINK ABOUT ONE FOR YOUR NEXT SESSION.

4: HOW WAS YOUR CLIENT RELATIONSHIP TODAY, WHY WAS THIS? WHAT WOULD YOU LIKE TO BE DIFFERENT?

5: WHAT TOOLS HAVE YOU USED TODAY, WHY? DID YOU PREPARE TO USE THEM? IF THIS IS THE CASE WHAT MIGHT YOU HAVE MISSED BY NOT PAYING ATTENTION? WHAT COULD YOU DO DIFFERENTLY NEXT TIME?

6: WHAT WAS YOUR STYLE TODAY? AUTOCRATIC (BOSSY AND AUTHORITIVE) DEMOCRATIC (GUIDE AND PERSONNEL), LAISSEZ-FAIRE (MINDFUL AND RELAXED). REFLECT ON THIS AND WATCH HOW YOU CHANGE, WHAT TRIGGERS YOUR STYLE?

7: HOW MUCH ACTIVE LISTENING DID YOU DO? DID YOU LISTEN TO UNDERSTAND OR LISTEN TO REPLY? A KEY ERROR IS A COACH FORMULATING THE NEXT QUESTION INSTEAD OF LISTENING.

8: IF YOU USED NO TOOLS OR TECHNIQUES TODAY HOW DID THAT MAKE YOU FEEL? DID YOU LEAVE THINKING YOU MISSED SOMETHING? WHAT COULD YOU CHANGE FOR NEXT TIME?

9: WHAT PERCENTAGE OF THE SESSION WAS DRIVEN BY YOU? HOW MUCH OF THE SESSION WERE YOU RELAXED AND NOTICED WHAT CAME UP IN THE SESSION?

10: HOW MUCH OF THE SESSION WAS ABOUT YOU AND HOW MUCH ABOUT THE CLIENT? HOW COULD YOU LOOK AT THIS IN MORE DETAIL?

DATE:-   /   /

1: HOW MUCH GUIDING VS TELLING DID YOU DO? WHO WAS THIS FOR YOU OR THE CLIENT? WHAT COULD YOU DO DIFFERENTLY TO GROW?

2: WHAT MODELS HAVE YOU USED TODAY? BEHAVIOURAL MODELS OR NOTICING EMOTIONS AND FEELINGS? WHAT COULD YOU THINK ABOUT DIFFERENTLY FOR THE NEXT SESSION?

3: HOW MUCH OF YOUR WORK IS A HABIT? WHAT NEW HABITS WOULD YOU LIKE TO CREATE AND WHAT ONES WOULD YOU LIKE TO DELETE LIKE AN APP ON YOUR PHONE. THINK ABOUT ONE FOR YOUR NEXT SESSION.

4: HOW WAS YOUR CLIENT RELATIONSHIP TODAY, WHY WAS THIS? WHAT WOULD YOU LIKE TO BE DIFFERENT?

5: WHAT TOOLS HAVE YOU USED TODAY, WHY? DID YOU PREPARE TO USE THEM? IF THIS IS THE CASE WHAT MIGHT YOU HAVE MISSED BY NOT PAYING ATTENTION? WHAT COULD YOU DO DIFFERENTLY NEXT TIME?

6: WHAT WAS YOUR STYLE TODAY? AUTOCRATIC (BOSSY AND AUTHORITIVE) DEMOCRATIC (GUIDE AND PERSONNEL), LAISSEZ-FAIRE (MINDFUL AND RELAXED). REFLECT ON THIS AND WATCH HOW YOU CHANGE, WHAT TRIGGERS YOUR STYLE?

7: HOW MUCH ACTIVE LISTENING DID YOU DO? DID YOU LISTEN TO UNDERSTAND OR LISTEN TO REPLY? A KEY ERROR IS A COACH FORMULATING THE NEXT QUESTION INSTEAD OF LISTENING.

8: IF YOU USED NO TOOLS OR TECHNIQUES TODAY HOW DID THAT MAKE YOU FEEL? DID YOU LEAVE THINKING YOU MISSED SOMETHING? WHAT COULD YOU CHANGE FOR NEXT TIME?

9: WHAT PERCENTAGE OF THE SESSION WAS DRIVEN BY YOU? HOW MUCH OF THE SESSION WERE YOU RELAXED AND NOTICED WHAT CAME UP IN THE SESSION?

10: HOW MUCH OF THE SESSION WAS ABOUT YOU AND HOW MUCH ABOUT THE CLIENT? HOW COULD YOU LOOK AT THIS IN MORE DETAIL?

DATE:-   /   /

1: HOW MUCH GUIDING VS TELLING DID YOU DO? WHO WAS THIS
FOR YOU OR THE CLIENT? WHAT COULD YOU DO DIFFERENTLY TO GROW?

2: WHAT MODELS HAVE YOU USED TODAY? BEHAVIOURAL MODELS OR
NOTICING EMOTIONS AND FEELINGS? WHAT COULD YOU THINK ABOUT
DIFFERENTLY FOR THE NEXT SESSION?

3: HOW MUCH OF YOUR WORK IS A HABIT? WHAT NEW HABITS WOULD
YOU LIKE TO CREATE AND WHAT ONES WOULD YOU LIKE TO DELETE LIKE
AN APP ON YOUR PHONE. THINK ABOUT ONE FOR YOUR NEXT SESSION.

4: HOW WAS YOUR CLIENT RELATIONSHIP TODAY, WHY WAS THIS?
WHAT WOULD YOU LIKE TO BE DIFFERENT?

5: WHAT TOOLS HAVE YOU USED TODAY, WHY? DID YOU PREPARE TO
USE THEM? IF THIS IS THE CASE WHAT MIGHT YOU HAVE MISSED BY NOT
PAYING ATTENTION? WHAT COULD YOU DO DIFFERENTLY NEXT TIME?

6: WHAT WAS YOUR STYLE TODAY? AUTOCRATIC (BOSSY AND AUTHORITIVE) DEMOCRATIC (GUIDE AND PERSONNEL), LAISSEZ-FAIRE (MINDFUL AND RELAXED). REFLECT ON THIS AND WATCH HOW YOU CHANGE, WHAT TRIGGERS YOUR STYLE?

7: HOW MUCH ACTIVE LISTENING DID YOU DO? DID YOU LISTEN TO UNDERSTAND OR LISTEN TO REPLY? A KEY ERROR IS A COACH FORMULATING THE NEXT QUESTION INSTEAD OF LISTENING.

8: IF YOU USED NO TOOLS OR TECHNIQUES TODAY HOW DID THAT MAKE YOU FEEL? DID YOU LEAVE THINKING YOU MISSED SOMETHING? WHAT COULD YOU CHANGE FOR NEXT TIME?

9: WHAT PERCENTAGE OF THE SESSION WAS DRIVEN BY YOU? HOW MUCH OF THE SESSION WERE YOU RELAXED AND NOTICED WHAT CAME UP IN THE SESSION?

10: HOW MUCH OF THE SESSION WAS ABOUT YOU AND HOW MUCH ABOUT THE CLIENT? HOW COULD YOU LOOK AT THIS IN MORE DETAIL?

DATE:-   /   /

1: HOW MUCH GUIDING VS TELLING DID YOU DO? WHO WAS THIS FOR YOU OR THE CLIENT? WHAT COULD YOU DO DIFFERENTLY TO GROW?

2: WHAT MODELS HAVE YOU USED TODAY? BEHAVIOURAL MODELS OR NOTICING EMOTIONS AND FEELINGS? WHAT COULD YOU THINK ABOUT DIFFERENTLY FOR THE NEXT SESSION?

3: HOW MUCH OF YOUR WORK IS A HABIT? WHAT NEW HABITS WOULD YOU LIKE TO CREATE AND WHAT ONES WOULD YOU LIKE TO DELETE LIKE AN APP ON YOUR PHONE. THINK ABOUT ONE FOR YOUR NEXT SESSION.

4: HOW WAS YOUR CLIENT RELATIONSHIP TODAY, WHY WAS THIS? WHAT WOULD YOU LIKE TO BE DIFFERENT?

5: WHAT TOOLS HAVE YOU USED TODAY, WHY? DID YOU PREPARE TO USE THEM? IF THIS IS THE CASE WHAT MIGHT YOU HAVE MISSED BY NOT PAYING ATTENTION? WHAT COULD YOU DO DIFFERENTLY NEXT TIME?

6: WHAT WAS YOUR STYLE TODAY? AUTOCRATIC (BOSSY AND AUTHORITIVE) DEMOCRATIC (GUIDE AND PERSONNEL), LAISSEZ-FAIRE (MINDFUL AND RELAXED). REFLECT ON THIS AND WATCH HOW YOU CHANGE, WHAT TRIGGERS YOUR STYLE?

7: HOW MUCH ACTIVE LISTENING DID YOU DO? DID YOU LISTEN TO UNDERSTAND OR LISTEN TO REPLY? A KEY ERROR IS A COACH FORMULATING THE NEXT QUESTION INSTEAD OF LISTENING.

8: IF YOU USED NO TOOLS OR TECHNIQUES TODAY HOW DID THAT MAKE YOU FEEL? DID YOU LEAVE THINKING YOU MISSED SOMETHING? WHAT COULD YOU CHANGE FOR NEXT TIME?

9: WHAT PERCENTAGE OF THE SESSION WAS DRIVEN BY YOU? HOW MUCH OF THE SESSION WERE YOU RELAXED AND NOTICED WHAT CAME UP IN THE SESSION?

10: HOW MUCH OF THE SESSION WAS ABOUT YOU AND HOW MUCH ABOUT THE CLIENT? HOW COULD YOU LOOK AT THIS IN MORE DETAIL?

DATE:-   /   /

1: HOW MUCH GUIDING VS TELLING DID YOU DO? WHO WAS THIS FOR YOU OR THE CLIENT? WHAT COULD YOU DO DIFFERENTLY TO GROW?

2: WHAT MODELS HAVE YOU USED TODAY? BEHAVIOURAL MODELS OR NOTICING EMOTIONS AND FEELINGS? WHAT COULD YOU THINK ABOUT DIFFERENTLY FOR THE NEXT SESSION?

3: HOW MUCH OF YOUR WORK IS A HABIT? WHAT NEW HABITS WOULD YOU LIKE TO CREATE AND WHAT ONES WOULD YOU LIKE TO DELETE LIKE AN APP ON YOUR PHONE. THINK ABOUT ONE FOR YOUR NEXT SESSION.

4: HOW WAS YOUR CLIENT RELATIONSHIP TODAY, WHY WAS THIS? WHAT WOULD YOU LIKE TO BE DIFFERENT?

5: WHAT TOOLS HAVE YOU USED TODAY, WHY? DID YOU PREPARE TO USE THEM? IF THIS IS THE CASE WHAT MIGHT YOU HAVE MISSED BY NOT PAYING ATTENTION? WHAT COULD YOU DO DIFFERENTLY NEXT TIME?

REFLECTION ON YOUR USE OF TOOLS AND TECHNIQUES IN COACHING

 DAY 9

6: WHAT WAS YOUR STYLE TODAY? AUTOCRATIC (BOSSY AND AUTHORITIVE) DEMOCRATIC (GUIDE AND PERSONNEL), LAISSEZ-FAIRE (MINDFUL AND RELAXED). REFLECT ON THIS AND WATCH HOW YOU CHANGE, WHAT TRIGGERS YOUR STYLE?

7: HOW MUCH ACTIVE LISTENING DID YOU DO? DID YOU LISTEN TO UNDERSTAND OR LISTEN TO REPLY? A KEY ERROR IS A COACH FORMULATING THE NEXT QUESTION INSTEAD OF LISTENING.

8: IF YOU USED NO TOOLS OR TECHNIQUES TODAY HOW DID THAT MAKE YOU FEEL? DID YOU LEAVE THINKING YOU MISSED SOMETHING? WHAT COULD YOU CHANGE FOR NEXT TIME?

9: WHAT PERCENTAGE OF THE SESSION WAS DRIVEN BY YOU? HOW MUCH OF THE SESSION WERE YOU RELAXED AND NOTICED WHAT CAME UP IN THE SESSION?

10: HOW MUCH OF THE SESSION WAS ABOUT YOU AND HOW MUCH ABOUT THE CLIENT? HOW COULD YOU LOOK AT THIS IN MORE DETAIL?

DATE:-   /   /

1: HOW MUCH GUIDING VS TELLING DID YOU DO? WHO WAS THIS
FOR YOU OR THE CLIENT? WHAT COULD YOU DO DIFFERENTLY TO GROW?

2: WHAT MODELS HAVE YOU USED TODAY? BEHAVIOURAL MODELS OR
NOTICING EMOTIONS AND FEELINGS? WHAT COULD YOU THINK ABOUT
DIFFERENTLY FOR THE NEXT SESSION?

3: HOW MUCH OF YOUR WORK IS A HABIT? WHAT NEW HABITS WOULD
YOU LIKE TO CREATE AND WHAT ONES WOULD YOU LIKE TO DELETE LIKE
AN APP ON YOUR PHONE. THINK ABOUT ONE FOR YOUR NEXT SESSION.

4: HOW WAS YOUR CLIENT RELATIONSHIP TODAY, WHY WAS THIS?
WHAT WOULD YOU LIKE TO BE DIFFERENT?

5: WHAT TOOLS HAVE YOU USED TODAY, WHY? DID YOU PREPARE TO
USE THEM? IF THIS IS THE CASE WHAT MIGHT YOU HAVE MISSED BY NOT
PAYING ATTENTION? WHAT COULD YOU DO DIFFERENTLY NEXT TIME?

6: WHAT WAS YOUR STYLE TODAY? AUTOCRATIC (BOSSY AND AUTHORITIVE) DEMOCRATIC (GUIDE AND PERSONNEL), LAISSEZ-FAIRE (MINDFUL AND RELAXED). REFLECT ON THIS AND WATCH HOW YOU CHANGE, WHAT TRIGGERS YOUR STYLE?

7: HOW MUCH ACTIVE LISTENING DID YOU DO? DID YOU LISTEN TO UNDERSTAND OR LISTEN TO REPLY? A KEY ERROR IS A COACH FORMULATING THE NEXT QUESTION INSTEAD OF LISTENING.

8: IF YOU USED NO TOOLS OR TECHNIQUES TODAY HOW DID THAT MAKE YOU FEEL? DID YOU LEAVE THINKING YOU MISSED SOMETHING? WHAT COULD YOU CHANGE FOR NEXT TIME?

9: WHAT PERCENTAGE OF THE SESSION WAS DRIVEN BY YOU? HOW MUCH OF THE SESSION WERE YOU RELAXED AND NOTICED WHAT CAME UP IN THE SESSION?

10: HOW MUCH OF THE SESSION WAS ABOUT YOU AND HOW MUCH ABOUT THE CLIENT? HOW COULD YOU LOOK AT THIS IN MORE DETAIL?

1: HOW HAVE I GROWN OVER THE LAST 10 DAYS

2: WHAT AM I GOING TO FOCUS ON OVER THE NEXT 10 DAYS?

3: WHAT FIVE THINGS AM I POSITIVELY TAKING FROM THE LAST 10 DAYS AND MOVING THEM FORWARD INTO THE NEXT 10 DAYS.

-
-
-
-
-

4: WHAT KEY AREAS WOULD I LIKE TO CONCENTRATE ON?

"Who, exactly, seeks out a coach? If you ask a coach the answer is usually the same: Winners who want even more out of life."

UNKNOWN

DATE:-   /   /

1: HOW MUCH GUIDING VS TELLING DID YOU DO? WHO WAS THIS
FOR YOU OR THE CLIENT? WHAT COULD YOU DO DIFFERENTLY TO GROW?

2: WHAT MODELS HAVE YOU USED TODAY? BEHAVIOURAL MODELS OR
NOTICING EMOTIONS AND FEELINGS? WHAT COULD YOU THINK ABOUT
DIFFERENTLY FOR THE NEXT SESSION?

3: HOW MUCH OF YOUR WORK IS A HABIT? WHAT NEW HABITS WOULD
YOU LIKE TO CREATE AND WHAT ONES WOULD YOU LIKE TO DELETE LIKE
AN APP ON YOUR PHONE. THINK ABOUT ONE FOR YOUR NEXT SESSION.

4: HOW WAS YOUR CLIENT RELATIONSHIP TODAY, WHY WAS THIS?
WHAT WOULD YOU LIKE TO BE DIFFERENT?

5: WHAT TOOLS HAVE YOU USED TODAY, WHY? DID YOU PREPARE TO
USE THEM? IF THIS IS THE CASE WHAT MIGHT YOU HAVE MISSED BY NOT
PAYING ATTENTION? WHAT COULD YOU DO DIFFERENTLY NEXT TIME?

6: WHAT WAS YOUR STYLE TODAY? AUTOCRATIC (BOSSY AND AUTHORITIVE) DEMOCRATIC (GUIDE AND PERSONNEL), LAISSEZ-FAIRE (MINDFUL AND RELAXED). REFLECT ON THIS AND WATCH HOW YOU CHANGE, WHAT TRIGGERS YOUR STYLE?

7: HOW MUCH ACTIVE LISTENING DID YOU DO? DID YOU LISTEN TO UNDERSTAND OR LISTEN TO REPLY? A KEY ERROR IS A COACH FORMULATING THE NEXT QUESTION INSTEAD OF LISTENING.

8: IF YOU USED NO TOOLS OR TECHNIQUES TODAY HOW DID THAT MAKE YOU FEEL? DID YOU LEAVE THINKING YOU MISSED SOMETHING? WHAT COULD YOU CHANGE FOR NEXT TIME?

9: WHAT PERCENTAGE OF THE SESSION WAS DRIVEN BY YOU? HOW MUCH OF THE SESSION WERE YOU RELAXED AND NOTICED WHAT CAME UP IN THE SESSION?

10: HOW MUCH OF THE SESSION WAS ABOUT YOU AND HOW MUCH ABOUT THE CLIENT? HOW COULD YOU LOOK AT THIS IN MORE DETAIL?

DATE:- / /

1: HOW MUCH GUIDING VS TELLING DID YOU DO? WHO WAS THIS FOR YOU OR THE CLIENT? WHAT COULD YOU DO DIFFERENTLY TO GROW?

2: WHAT MODELS HAVE YOU USED TODAY? BEHAVIOURAL MODELS OR NOTICING EMOTIONS AND FEELINGS? WHAT COULD YOU THINK ABOUT DIFFERENTLY FOR THE NEXT SESSION?

3: HOW MUCH OF YOUR WORK IS A HABIT? WHAT NEW HABITS WOULD YOU LIKE TO CREATE AND WHAT ONES WOULD YOU LIKE TO DELETE LIKE AN APP ON YOUR PHONE. THINK ABOUT ONE FOR YOUR NEXT SESSION.

4: HOW WAS YOUR CLIENT RELATIONSHIP TODAY, WHY WAS THIS? WHAT WOULD YOU LIKE TO BE DIFFERENT?

5: WHAT TOOLS HAVE YOU USED TODAY, WHY? DID YOU PREPARE TO USE THEM? IF THIS IS THE CASE WHAT MIGHT YOU HAVE MISSED BY NOT PAYING ATTENTION? WHAT COULD YOU DO DIFFERENTLY NEXT TIME?

6: WHAT WAS YOUR STYLE TODAY? AUTOCRATIC (BOSSY AND AUTHORITIVE) DEMOCRATIC (GUIDE AND PERSONNEL), LAISSEZ-FAIRE (MINDFUL AND RELAXED). REFLECT ON THIS AND WATCH HOW YOU CHANGE, WHAT TRIGGERS YOUR STYLE?

7: HOW MUCH ACTIVE LISTENING DID YOU DO? DID YOU LISTEN TO UNDERSTAND OR LISTEN TO REPLY? A KEY ERROR IS A COACH FORMULATING THE NEXT QUESTION INSTEAD OF LISTENING.

8: IF YOU USED NO TOOLS OR TECHNIQUES TODAY HOW DID THAT MAKE YOU FEEL? DID YOU LEAVE THINKING YOU MISSED SOMETHING? WHAT COULD YOU CHANGE FOR NEXT TIME?

9: WHAT PERCENTAGE OF THE SESSION WAS DRIVEN BY YOU? HOW MUCH OF THE SESSION WERE YOU RELAXED AND NOTICED WHAT CAME UP IN THE SESSION?

10: HOW MUCH OF THE SESSION WAS ABOUT YOU AND HOW MUCH ABOUT THE CLIENT? HOW COULD YOU LOOK AT THIS IN MORE DETAIL?

DATE:-   /   /

**1: HOW MUCH GUIDING VS TELLING DID YOU DO? WHO WAS THIS
FOR YOU OR THE CLIENT? WHAT COULD YOU DO DIFFERENTLY TO GROW?**

**2: WHAT MODELS HAVE YOU USED TODAY? BEHAVIOURAL MODELS OR
NOTICING EMOTIONS AND FEELINGS? WHAT COULD YOU THINK ABOUT
DIFFERENTLY FOR THE NEXT SESSION?**

**3: HOW MUCH OF YOUR WORK IS A HABIT? WHAT NEW HABITS WOULD
YOU LIKE TO CREATE AND WHAT ONES WOULD YOU LIKE TO DELETE LIKE
AN APP ON YOUR PHONE. THINK ABOUT ONE FOR YOUR NEXT SESSION.**

**4: HOW WAS YOUR CLIENT RELATIONSHIP TODAY, WHY WAS THIS?
WHAT WOULD YOU LIKE TO BE DIFFERENT?**

**5: WHAT TOOLS HAVE YOU USED TODAY, WHY? DID YOU PREPARE TO
USE THEM? IF THIS IS THE CASE WHAT MIGHT YOU HAVE MISSED BY NOT
PAYING ATTENTION? WHAT COULD YOU DO DIFFERENTLY NEXT TIME?**

6: WHAT WAS YOUR STYLE TODAY? AUTOCRATIC (BOSSY AND AUTHORITIVE) DEMOCRATIC (GUIDE AND PERSONNEL), LAISSEZ-FAIRE (MINDFUL AND RELAXED). REFLECT ON THIS AND WATCH HOW YOU CHANGE, WHAT TRIGGERS YOUR STYLE?

7: HOW MUCH ACTIVE LISTENING DID YOU DO? DID YOU LISTEN TO UNDERSTAND OR LISTEN TO REPLY? A KEY ERROR IS A COACH FORMULATING THE NEXT QUESTION INSTEAD OF LISTENING.

8: IF YOU USED NO TOOLS OR TECHNIQUES TODAY HOW DID THAT MAKE YOU FEEL? DID YOU LEAVE THINKING YOU MISSED SOMETHING? WHAT COULD YOU CHANGE FOR NEXT TIME?

9: WHAT PERCENTAGE OF THE SESSION WAS DRIVEN BY YOU? HOW MUCH OF THE SESSION WERE YOU RELAXED AND NOTICED WHAT CAME UP IN THE SESSION?

10: HOW MUCH OF THE SESSION WAS ABOUT YOU AND HOW MUCH ABOUT THE CLIENT? HOW COULD YOU LOOK AT THIS IN MORE DETAIL?

DATE:-   /   /

1: HOW MUCH GUIDING VS TELLING DID YOU DO? WHO WAS THIS FOR YOU OR THE CLIENT? WHAT COULD YOU DO DIFFERENTLY TO GROW?

2: WHAT MODELS HAVE YOU USED TODAY? BEHAVIOURAL MODELS OR NOTICING EMOTIONS AND FEELINGS? WHAT COULD YOU THINK ABOUT DIFFERENTLY FOR THE NEXT SESSION?

3: HOW MUCH OF YOUR WORK IS A HABIT? WHAT NEW HABITS WOULD YOU LIKE TO CREATE AND WHAT ONES WOULD YOU LIKE TO DELETE LIKE AN APP ON YOUR PHONE. THINK ABOUT ONE FOR YOUR NEXT SESSION.

4: HOW WAS YOUR CLIENT RELATIONSHIP TODAY, WHY WAS THIS? WHAT WOULD YOU LIKE TO BE DIFFERENT?

5: WHAT TOOLS HAVE YOU USED TODAY, WHY? DID YOU PREPARE TO USE THEM? IF THIS IS THE CASE WHAT MIGHT YOU HAVE MISSED BY NOT PAYING ATTENTION? WHAT COULD YOU DO DIFFERENTLY NEXT TIME?

REFLECTION ON YOUR USE OF TOOLS AND TECHNIQUES IN COACHING

6: WHAT WAS YOUR STYLE TODAY? AUTOCRATIC (BOSSY AND AUTHORITIVE) DEMOCRATIC (GUIDE AND PERSONNEL), LAISSEZ-FAIRE (MINDFUL AND RELAXED). REFLECT ON THIS AND WATCH HOW YOU CHANGE, WHAT TRIGGERS YOUR STYLE?

7: HOW MUCH ACTIVE LISTENING DID YOU DO? DID YOU LISTEN TO UNDERSTAND OR LISTEN TO REPLY? A KEY ERROR IS A COACH FORMULATING THE NEXT QUESTION INSTEAD OF LISTENING.

8: IF YOU USED NO TOOLS OR TECHNIQUES TODAY HOW DID THAT MAKE YOU FEEL? DID YOU LEAVE THINKING YOU MISSED SOMETHING? WHAT COULD YOU CHANGE FOR NEXT TIME?

9: WHAT PERCENTAGE OF THE SESSION WAS DRIVEN BY YOU? HOW MUCH OF THE SESSION WERE YOU RELAXED AND NOTICED WHAT CAME UP IN THE SESSION?

10: HOW MUCH OF THE SESSION WAS ABOUT YOU AND HOW MUCH ABOUT THE CLIENT? HOW COULD YOU LOOK AT THIS IN MORE DETAIL?

DATE:-   /   /

1: HOW MUCH GUIDING VS TELLING DID YOU DO? WHO WAS THIS FOR YOU OR THE CLIENT? WHAT COULD YOU DO DIFFERENTLY TO GROW?

2: WHAT MODELS HAVE YOU USED TODAY? BEHAVIOURAL MODELS OR NOTICING EMOTIONS AND FEELINGS? WHAT COULD YOU THINK ABOUT DIFFERENTLY FOR THE NEXT SESSION?

3: HOW MUCH OF YOUR WORK IS A HABIT? WHAT NEW HABITS WOULD YOU LIKE TO CREATE AND WHAT ONES WOULD YOU LIKE TO DELETE LIKE AN APP ON YOUR PHONE. THINK ABOUT ONE FOR YOUR NEXT SESSION.

4: HOW WAS YOUR CLIENT RELATIONSHIP TODAY, WHY WAS THIS? WHAT WOULD YOU LIKE TO BE DIFFERENT?

5: WHAT TOOLS HAVE YOU USED TODAY, WHY? DID YOU PREPARE TO USE THEM? IF THIS IS THE CASE WHAT MIGHT YOU HAVE MISSED BY NOT PAYING ATTENTION? WHAT COULD YOU DO DIFFERENTLY NEXT TIME?

6: WHAT WAS YOUR STYLE TODAY? AUTOCRATIC (BOSSY AND AUTHORITIVE) DEMOCRATIC (GUIDE AND PERSONNEL), LAISSEZ-FAIRE (MINDFUL AND RELAXED). REFLECT ON THIS AND WATCH HOW YOU CHANGE, WHAT TRIGGERS YOUR STYLE?

7: HOW MUCH ACTIVE LISTENING DID YOU DO? DID YOU LISTEN TO UNDERSTAND OR LISTEN TO REPLY? A KEY ERROR IS A COACH FORMULATING THE NEXT QUESTION INSTEAD OF LISTENING.

8: IF YOU USED NO TOOLS OR TECHNIQUES TODAY HOW DID THAT MAKE YOU FEEL? DID YOU LEAVE THINKING YOU MISSED SOMETHING? WHAT COULD YOU CHANGE FOR NEXT TIME?

9: WHAT PERCENTAGE OF THE SESSION WAS DRIVEN BY YOU? HOW MUCH OF THE SESSION WERE YOU RELAXED AND NOTICED WHAT CAME UP IN THE SESSION?

10: HOW MUCH OF THE SESSION WAS ABOUT YOU AND HOW MUCH ABOUT THE CLIENT? HOW COULD YOU LOOK AT THIS IN MORE DETAIL?

DATE:-   /   /

1: HOW MUCH GUIDING VS TELLING DID YOU DO? WHO WAS THIS
FOR YOU OR THE CLIENT? WHAT COULD YOU DO DIFFERENTLY TO GROW?

2: WHAT MODELS HAVE YOU USED TODAY? BEHAVIOURAL MODELS OR
NOTICING EMOTIONS AND FEELINGS? WHAT COULD YOU THINK ABOUT
DIFFERENTLY FOR THE NEXT SESSION?

3: HOW MUCH OF YOUR WORK IS A HABIT? WHAT NEW HABITS WOULD
YOU LIKE TO CREATE AND WHAT ONES WOULD YOU LIKE TO DELETE LIKE
AN APP ON YOUR PHONE. THINK ABOUT ONE FOR YOUR NEXT SESSION.

4: HOW WAS YOUR CLIENT RELATIONSHIP TODAY, WHY WAS THIS?
WHAT WOULD YOU LIKE TO BE DIFFERENT?

5: WHAT TOOLS HAVE YOU USED TODAY, WHY? DID YOU PREPARE TO
USE THEM? IF THIS IS THE CASE WHAT MIGHT YOU HAVE MISSED BY NOT
PAYING ATTENTION? WHAT COULD YOU DO DIFFERENTLY NEXT TIME?

6: WHAT WAS YOUR STYLE TODAY? AUTOCRATIC (BOSSY AND AUTHORITIVE) DEMOCRATIC (GUIDE AND PERSONNEL), LAISSEZ-FAIRE (MINDFUL AND RELAXED). REFLECT ON THIS AND WATCH HOW YOU CHANGE, WHAT TRIGGERS YOUR STYLE?

7: HOW MUCH ACTIVE LISTENING DID YOU DO? DID YOU LISTEN TO UNDERSTAND OR LISTEN TO REPLY? A KEY ERROR IS A COACH FORMULATING THE NEXT QUESTION INSTEAD OF LISTENING.

8: IF YOU USED NO TOOLS OR TECHNIQUES TODAY HOW DID THAT MAKE YOU FEEL? DID YOU LEAVE THINKING YOU MISSED SOMETHING? WHAT COULD YOU CHANGE FOR NEXT TIME?

9: WHAT PERCENTAGE OF THE SESSION WAS DRIVEN BY YOU? HOW MUCH OF THE SESSION WERE YOU RELAXED AND NOTICED WHAT CAME UP IN THE SESSION?

10: HOW MUCH OF THE SESSION WAS ABOUT YOU AND HOW MUCH ABOUT THE CLIENT? HOW COULD YOU LOOK AT THIS IN MORE DETAIL?

DATE:-   /   /

1: HOW MUCH GUIDING VS TELLING DID YOU DO? WHO WAS THIS FOR YOU OR THE CLIENT? WHAT COULD YOU DO DIFFERENTLY TO GROW?

2: WHAT MODELS HAVE YOU USED TODAY? BEHAVIOURAL MODELS OR NOTICING EMOTIONS AND FEELINGS? WHAT COULD YOU THINK ABOUT DIFFERENTLY FOR THE NEXT SESSION?

3: HOW MUCH OF YOUR WORK IS A HABIT? WHAT NEW HABITS WOULD YOU LIKE TO CREATE AND WHAT ONES WOULD YOU LIKE TO DELETE LIKE AN APP ON YOUR PHONE. THINK ABOUT ONE FOR YOUR NEXT SESSION.

4: HOW WAS YOUR CLIENT RELATIONSHIP TODAY, WHY WAS THIS? WHAT WOULD YOU LIKE TO BE DIFFERENT?

5: WHAT TOOLS HAVE YOU USED TODAY, WHY? DID YOU PREPARE TO USE THEM? IF THIS IS THE CASE WHAT MIGHT YOU HAVE MISSED BY NOT PAYING ATTENTION? WHAT COULD YOU DO DIFFERENTLY NEXT TIME?

6: WHAT WAS YOUR STYLE TODAY? AUTOCRATIC (BOSSY AND AUTHORITIVE) DEMOCRATIC (GUIDE AND PERSONNEL), LAISSEZ-FAIRE (MINDFUL AND RELAXED). REFLECT ON THIS AND WATCH HOW YOU CHANGE, WHAT TRIGGERS YOUR STYLE?

7: HOW MUCH ACTIVE LISTENING DID YOU DO? DID YOU LISTEN TO UNDERSTAND OR LISTEN TO REPLY? A KEY ERROR IS A COACH FORMULATING THE NEXT QUESTION INSTEAD OF LISTENING.

8: IF YOU USED NO TOOLS OR TECHNIQUES TODAY HOW DID THAT MAKE YOU FEEL? DID YOU LEAVE THINKING YOU MISSED SOMETHING? WHAT COULD YOU CHANGE FOR NEXT TIME?

9: WHAT PERCENTAGE OF THE SESSION WAS DRIVEN BY YOU? HOW MUCH OF THE SESSION WERE YOU RELAXED AND NOTICED WHAT CAME UP IN THE SESSION?

10: HOW MUCH OF THE SESSION WAS ABOUT YOU AND HOW MUCH ABOUT THE CLIENT? HOW COULD YOU LOOK AT THIS IN MORE DETAIL?

DATE:-   /   /

1: HOW MUCH GUIDING VS TELLING DID YOU DO? WHO WAS THIS FOR YOU OR THE CLIENT? WHAT COULD YOU DO DIFFERENTLY TO GROW?

2: WHAT MODELS HAVE YOU USED TODAY? BEHAVIOURAL MODELS OR NOTICING EMOTIONS AND FEELINGS? WHAT COULD YOU THINK ABOUT DIFFERENTLY FOR THE NEXT SESSION?

3: HOW MUCH OF YOUR WORK IS A HABIT? WHAT NEW HABITS WOULD YOU LIKE TO CREATE AND WHAT ONES WOULD YOU LIKE TO DELETE LIKE AN APP ON YOUR PHONE. THINK ABOUT ONE FOR YOUR NEXT SESSION.

4: HOW WAS YOUR CLIENT RELATIONSHIP TODAY, WHY WAS THIS? WHAT WOULD YOU LIKE TO BE DIFFERENT?

5: WHAT TOOLS HAVE YOU USED TODAY, WHY? DID YOU PREPARE TO USE THEM? IF THIS IS THE CASE WHAT MIGHT YOU HAVE MISSED BY NOT PAYING ATTENTION? WHAT COULD YOU DO DIFFERENTLY NEXT TIME?

6: WHAT WAS YOUR STYLE TODAY? AUTOCRATIC (BOSSY AND AUTHORITIVE) DEMOCRATIC (GUIDE AND PERSONNEL), LAISSEZ-FAIRE (MINDFUL AND RELAXED). REFLECT ON THIS AND WATCH HOW YOU CHANGE, WHAT TRIGGERS YOUR STYLE?

7: HOW MUCH ACTIVE LISTENING DID YOU DO? DID YOU LISTEN TO UNDERSTAND OR LISTEN TO REPLY? A KEY ERROR IS A COACH FORMULATING THE NEXT QUESTION INSTEAD OF LISTENING.

8: IF YOU USED NO TOOLS OR TECHNIQUES TODAY HOW DID THAT MAKE YOU FEEL? DID YOU LEAVE THINKING YOU MISSED SOMETHING? WHAT COULD YOU CHANGE FOR NEXT TIME?

9: WHAT PERCENTAGE OF THE SESSION WAS DRIVEN BY YOU? HOW MUCH OF THE SESSION WERE YOU RELAXED AND NOTICED WHAT CAME UP IN THE SESSION?

10: HOW MUCH OF THE SESSION WAS ABOUT YOU AND HOW MUCH ABOUT THE CLIENT? HOW COULD YOU LOOK AT THIS IN MORE DETAIL?

DATE:-   /   /

1: HOW MUCH GUIDING VS TELLING DID YOU DO? WHO WAS THIS FOR YOU OR THE CLIENT? WHAT COULD YOU DO DIFFERENTLY TO GROW?

2: WHAT MODELS HAVE YOU USED TODAY? BEHAVIOURAL MODELS OR NOTICING EMOTIONS AND FEELINGS? WHAT COULD YOU THINK ABOUT DIFFERENTLY FOR THE NEXT SESSION?

3: HOW MUCH OF YOUR WORK IS A HABIT? WHAT NEW HABITS WOULD YOU LIKE TO CREATE AND WHAT ONES WOULD YOU LIKE TO DELETE LIKE AN APP ON YOUR PHONE. THINK ABOUT ONE FOR YOUR NEXT SESSION.

4: HOW WAS YOUR CLIENT RELATIONSHIP TODAY, WHY WAS THIS? WHAT WOULD YOU LIKE TO BE DIFFERENT?

5: WHAT TOOLS HAVE YOU USED TODAY, WHY? DID YOU PREPARE TO USE THEM? IF THIS IS THE CASE WHAT MIGHT YOU HAVE MISSED BY NOT PAYING ATTENTION? WHAT COULD YOU DO DIFFERENTLY NEXT TIME?

6: WHAT WAS YOUR STYLE TODAY? AUTOCRATIC (BOSSY AND AUTHORITIVE) DEMOCRATIC (GUIDE AND PERSONNEL), LAISSEZ-FAIRE (MINDFUL AND RELAXED). REFLECT ON THIS AND WATCH HOW YOU CHANGE, WHAT TRIGGERS YOUR STYLE?

7: HOW MUCH ACTIVE LISTENING DID YOU DO? DID YOU LISTEN TO UNDERSTAND OR LISTEN TO REPLY? A KEY ERROR IS A COACH FORMULATING THE NEXT QUESTION INSTEAD OF LISTENING.

8: IF YOU USED NO TOOLS OR TECHNIQUES TODAY HOW DID THAT MAKE YOU FEEL? DID YOU LEAVE THINKING YOU MISSED SOMETHING? WHAT COULD YOU CHANGE FOR NEXT TIME?

9: WHAT PERCENTAGE OF THE SESSION WAS DRIVEN BY YOU? HOW MUCH OF THE SESSION WERE YOU RELAXED AND NOTICED WHAT CAME UP IN THE SESSION?

10: HOW MUCH OF THE SESSION WAS ABOUT YOU AND HOW MUCH ABOUT THE CLIENT? HOW COULD YOU LOOK AT THIS IN MORE DETAIL?

DATE:-   /   /

1: HOW MUCH GUIDING VS TELLING DID YOU DO? WHO WAS THIS FOR YOU OR THE CLIENT? WHAT COULD YOU DO DIFFERENTLY TO GROW?

2: WHAT MODELS HAVE YOU USED TODAY? BEHAVIOURAL MODELS OR NOTICING EMOTIONS AND FEELINGS? WHAT COULD YOU THINK ABOUT DIFFERENTLY FOR THE NEXT SESSION?

3: HOW MUCH OF YOUR WORK IS A HABIT? WHAT NEW HABITS WOULD YOU LIKE TO CREATE AND WHAT ONES WOULD YOU LIKE TO DELETE LIKE AN APP ON YOUR PHONE. THINK ABOUT ONE FOR YOUR NEXT SESSION.

4: HOW WAS YOUR CLIENT RELATIONSHIP TODAY, WHY WAS THIS? WHAT WOULD YOU LIKE TO BE DIFFERENT?

5: WHAT TOOLS HAVE YOU USED TODAY, WHY? DID YOU PREPARE TO USE THEM? IF THIS IS THE CASE WHAT MIGHT YOU HAVE MISSED BY NOT PAYING ATTENTION? WHAT COULD YOU DO DIFFERENTLY NEXT TIME?

6: WHAT WAS YOUR STYLE TODAY? AUTOCRATIC (BOSSY AND AUTHORITIVE) DEMOCRATIC (GUIDE AND PERSONNEL), LAISSEZ-FAIRE (MINDFUL AND RELAXED). REFLECT ON THIS AND WATCH HOW YOU CHANGE, WHAT TRIGGERS YOUR STYLE?

7: HOW MUCH ACTIVE LISTENING DID YOU DO? DID YOU LISTEN TO UNDERSTAND OR LISTEN TO REPLY? A KEY ERROR IS A COACH FORMULATING THE NEXT QUESTION INSTEAD OF LISTENING.

8: IF YOU USED NO TOOLS OR TECHNIQUES TODAY HOW DID THAT MAKE YOU FEEL? DID YOU LEAVE THINKING YOU MISSED SOMETHING? WHAT COULD YOU CHANGE FOR NEXT TIME?

9: WHAT PERCENTAGE OF THE SESSION WAS DRIVEN BY YOU? HOW MUCH OF THE SESSION WERE YOU RELAXED AND NOTICED WHAT CAME UP IN THE SESSION?

10: HOW MUCH OF THE SESSION WAS ABOUT YOU AND HOW MUCH ABOUT THE CLIENT? HOW COULD YOU LOOK AT THIS IN MORE DETAIL?

1: HOW HAVE I GROWN OVER THE LAST 10 DAYS

2: WHAT AM I GOING TO FOCUS ON OVER THE NEXT 10 DAYS?

3: WHAT FIVE THINGS AM I POSITIVELY TAKING FROM THE LAST 10 DAYS AND MOVING THEM FORWARD INTO THE NEXT 10 DAYS.

-
-
-
-
-

4: WHAT KEY AREAS WOULD I LIKE TO CONCENTRATE ON?

"When you encourage others, you in the process are being encouraged because you're making a commitment to that person's life. Encouragement really does make a difference."

ZIG ZIGLAR

_____

_____

_____

_____

_____

_____

_____

_____

_____

_____

_____

_____

_____

DATE:-   /   /

1: HOW MUCH GUIDING VS TELLING DID YOU DO? WHO WAS THIS FOR YOU OR THE CLIENT? WHAT COULD YOU DO DIFFERENTLY TO GROW?

2: WHAT MODELS HAVE YOU USED TODAY? BEHAVIOURAL MODELS OR NOTICING EMOTIONS AND FEELINGS? WHAT COULD YOU THINK ABOUT DIFFERENTLY FOR THE NEXT SESSION?

3: HOW MUCH OF YOUR WORK IS A HABIT? WHAT NEW HABITS WOULD YOU LIKE TO CREATE AND WHAT ONES WOULD YOU LIKE TO DELETE LIKE AN APP ON YOUR PHONE. THINK ABOUT ONE FOR YOUR NEXT SESSION.

4: HOW WAS YOUR CLIENT RELATIONSHIP TODAY, WHY WAS THIS? WHAT WOULD YOU LIKE TO BE DIFFERENT?

5: WHAT TOOLS HAVE YOU USED TODAY, WHY? DID YOU PREPARE TO USE THEM? IF THIS IS THE CASE WHAT MIGHT YOU HAVE MISSED BY NOT PAYING ATTENTION? WHAT COULD YOU DO DIFFERENTLY NEXT TIME?

6: WHAT WAS YOUR STYLE TODAY? AUTOCRATIC (BOSSY AND AUTHORITIVE) DEMOCRATIC (GUIDE AND PERSONNEL), LAISSEZ-FAIRE (MINDFUL AND RELAXED). REFLECT ON THIS AND WATCH HOW YOU CHANGE, WHAT TRIGGERS YOUR STYLE?

7: HOW MUCH ACTIVE LISTENING DID YOU DO? DID YOU LISTEN TO UNDERSTAND OR LISTEN TO REPLY? A KEY ERROR IS A COACH FORMULATING THE NEXT QUESTION INSTEAD OF LISTENING.

8: IF YOU USED NO TOOLS OR TECHNIQUES TODAY HOW DID THAT MAKE YOU FEEL? DID YOU LEAVE THINKING YOU MISSED SOMETHING? WHAT COULD YOU CHANGE FOR NEXT TIME?

9: WHAT PERCENTAGE OF THE SESSION WAS DRIVEN BY YOU? HOW MUCH OF THE SESSION WERE YOU RELAXED AND NOTICED WHAT CAME UP IN THE SESSION?

10: HOW MUCH OF THE SESSION WAS ABOUT YOU AND HOW MUCH ABOUT THE CLIENT? HOW COULD YOU LOOK AT THIS IN MORE DETAIL?

DATE:-   /   /

1: HOW MUCH GUIDING VS TELLING DID YOU DO? WHO WAS THIS FOR YOU OR THE CLIENT? WHAT COULD YOU DO DIFFERENTLY TO GROW?

2: WHAT MODELS HAVE YOU USED TODAY? BEHAVIOURAL MODELS OR NOTICING EMOTIONS AND FEELINGS? WHAT COULD YOU THINK ABOUT DIFFERENTLY FOR THE NEXT SESSION?

3: HOW MUCH OF YOUR WORK IS A HABIT? WHAT NEW HABITS WOULD YOU LIKE TO CREATE AND WHAT ONES WOULD YOU LIKE TO DELETE LIKE AN APP ON YOUR PHONE. THINK ABOUT ONE FOR YOUR NEXT SESSION.

4: HOW WAS YOUR CLIENT RELATIONSHIP TODAY, WHY WAS THIS? WHAT WOULD YOU LIKE TO BE DIFFERENT?

5: WHAT TOOLS HAVE YOU USED TODAY, WHY? DID YOU PREPARE TO USE THEM? IF THIS IS THE CASE WHAT MIGHT YOU HAVE MISSED BY NOT PAYING ATTENTION? WHAT COULD YOU DO DIFFERENTLY NEXT TIME?

6: WHAT WAS YOUR STYLE TODAY? AUTOCRATIC (BOSSY AND AUTHORITIVE) DEMOCRATIC (GUIDE AND PERSONNEL), LAISSEZ-FAIRE (MINDFUL AND RELAXED). REFLECT ON THIS AND WATCH HOW YOU CHANGE, WHAT TRIGGERS YOUR STYLE?

7: HOW MUCH ACTIVE LISTENING DID YOU DO? DID YOU LISTEN TO UNDERSTAND OR LISTEN TO REPLY? A KEY ERROR IS A COACH FORMULATING THE NEXT QUESTION INSTEAD OF LISTENING.

8: IF YOU USED NO TOOLS OR TECHNIQUES TODAY HOW DID THAT MAKE YOU FEEL? DID YOU LEAVE THINKING YOU MISSED SOMETHING? WHAT COULD YOU CHANGE FOR NEXT TIME?

9: WHAT PERCENTAGE OF THE SESSION WAS DRIVEN BY YOU? HOW MUCH OF THE SESSION WERE YOU RELAXED AND NOTICED WHAT CAME UP IN THE SESSION?

10: HOW MUCH OF THE SESSION WAS ABOUT YOU AND HOW MUCH ABOUT THE CLIENT? HOW COULD YOU LOOK AT THIS IN MORE DETAIL?

DATE:-   /   /

1: HOW MUCH GUIDING VS TELLING DID YOU DO? WHO WAS THIS FOR YOU OR THE CLIENT? WHAT COULD YOU DO DIFFERENTLY TO GROW?

2: WHAT MODELS HAVE YOU USED TODAY? BEHAVIOURAL MODELS OR NOTICING EMOTIONS AND FEELINGS? WHAT COULD YOU THINK ABOUT DIFFERENTLY FOR THE NEXT SESSION?

3: HOW MUCH OF YOUR WORK IS A HABIT? WHAT NEW HABITS WOULD YOU LIKE TO CREATE AND WHAT ONES WOULD YOU LIKE TO DELETE LIKE AN APP ON YOUR PHONE. THINK ABOUT ONE FOR YOUR NEXT SESSION.

4: HOW WAS YOUR CLIENT RELATIONSHIP TODAY, WHY WAS THIS? WHAT WOULD YOU LIKE TO BE DIFFERENT?

5: WHAT TOOLS HAVE YOU USED TODAY, WHY? DID YOU PREPARE TO USE THEM? IF THIS IS THE CASE WHAT MIGHT YOU HAVE MISSED BY NOT PAYING ATTENTION? WHAT COULD YOU DO DIFFERENTLY NEXT TIME?

REFLECTION ON YOUR USE OF TOOLS AND TECHNIQUES IN COACHING

DAY 23

6: WHAT WAS YOUR STYLE TODAY? AUTOCRATIC (BOSSY AND AUTHORITIVE) DEMOCRATIC (GUIDE AND PERSONNEL), LAISSEZ-FAIRE (MINDFUL AND RELAXED). REFLECT ON THIS AND WATCH HOW YOU CHANGE, WHAT TRIGGERS YOUR STYLE?

7: HOW MUCH ACTIVE LISTENING DID YOU DO? DID YOU LISTEN TO UNDERSTAND OR LISTEN TO REPLY? A KEY ERROR IS A COACH FORMULATING THE NEXT QUESTION INSTEAD OF LISTENING.

8: IF YOU USED NO TOOLS OR TECHNIQUES TODAY HOW DID THAT MAKE YOU FEEL? DID YOU LEAVE THINKING YOU MISSED SOMETHING? WHAT COULD YOU CHANGE FOR NEXT TIME?

9: WHAT PERCENTAGE OF THE SESSION WAS DRIVEN BY YOU? HOW MUCH OF THE SESSION WERE YOU RELAXED AND NOTICED WHAT CAME UP IN THE SESSION?

10: HOW MUCH OF THE SESSION WAS ABOUT YOU AND HOW MUCH ABOUT THE CLIENT? HOW COULD YOU LOOK AT THIS IN MORE DETAIL?

DATE:- / /

1: HOW MUCH GUIDING VS TELLING DID YOU DO? WHO WAS THIS
FOR YOU OR THE CLIENT? WHAT COULD YOU DO DIFFERENTLY TO GROW?

2: WHAT MODELS HAVE YOU USED TODAY? BEHAVIOURAL MODELS OR
NOTICING EMOTIONS AND FEELINGS? WHAT COULD YOU THINK ABOUT
DIFFERENTLY FOR THE NEXT SESSION?

3: HOW MUCH OF YOUR WORK IS A HABIT? WHAT NEW HABITS WOULD
YOU LIKE TO CREATE AND WHAT ONES WOULD YOU LIKE TO DELETE LIKE
AN APP ON YOUR PHONE. THINK ABOUT ONE FOR YOUR NEXT SESSION.

4: HOW WAS YOUR CLIENT RELATIONSHIP TODAY, WHY WAS THIS?
WHAT WOULD YOU LIKE TO BE DIFFERENT?

5: WHAT TOOLS HAVE YOU USED TODAY, WHY? DID YOU PREPARE TO
USE THEM? IF THIS IS THE CASE WHAT MIGHT YOU HAVE MISSED BY NOT
PAYING ATTENTION? WHAT COULD YOU DO DIFFERENTLY NEXT TIME?

6: WHAT WAS YOUR STYLE TODAY? AUTOCRATIC (BOSSY AND AUTHORITIVE) DEMOCRATIC (GUIDE AND PERSONNEL), LAISSEZ-FAIRE (MINDFUL AND RELAXED). REFLECT ON THIS AND WATCH HOW YOU CHANGE, WHAT TRIGGERS YOUR STYLE?

7: HOW MUCH ACTIVE LISTENING DID YOU DO? DID YOU LISTEN TO UNDERSTAND OR LISTEN TO REPLY? A KEY ERROR IS A COACH FORMULATING THE NEXT QUESTION INSTEAD OF LISTENING.

8: IF YOU USED NO TOOLS OR TECHNIQUES TODAY HOW DID THAT MAKE YOU FEEL? DID YOU LEAVE THINKING YOU MISSED SOMETHING? WHAT COULD YOU CHANGE FOR NEXT TIME?

9: WHAT PERCENTAGE OF THE SESSION WAS DRIVEN BY YOU? HOW MUCH OF THE SESSION WERE YOU RELAXED AND NOTICED WHAT CAME UP IN THE SESSION?

10: HOW MUCH OF THE SESSION WAS ABOUT YOU AND HOW MUCH ABOUT THE CLIENT? HOW COULD YOU LOOK AT THIS IN MORE DETAIL?

DATE:-   /   /

**1: HOW MUCH GUIDING VS TELLING DID YOU DO? WHO WAS THIS
FOR YOU OR THE CLIENT? WHAT COULD YOU DO DIFFERENTLY TO GROW?**

**2: WHAT MODELS HAVE YOU USED TODAY? BEHAVIOURAL MODELS OR
NOTICING EMOTIONS AND FEELINGS? WHAT COULD YOU THINK ABOUT
DIFFERENTLY FOR THE NEXT SESSION?**

**3: HOW MUCH OF YOUR WORK IS A HABIT? WHAT NEW HABITS WOULD
YOU LIKE TO CREATE AND WHAT ONES WOULD YOU LIKE TO DELETE LIKE
AN APP ON YOUR PHONE. THINK ABOUT ONE FOR YOUR NEXT SESSION.**

**4: HOW WAS YOUR CLIENT RELATIONSHIP TODAY, WHY WAS THIS?
WHAT WOULD YOU LIKE TO BE DIFFERENT?**

**5: WHAT TOOLS HAVE YOU USED TODAY, WHY? DID YOU PREPARE TO
USE THEM? IF THIS IS THE CASE WHAT MIGHT YOU HAVE MISSED BY NOT
PAYING ATTENTION? WHAT COULD YOU DO DIFFERENTLY NEXT TIME?**

6: WHAT WAS YOUR STYLE TODAY? AUTOCRATIC (BOSSY AND AUTHORITIVE) DEMOCRATIC (GUIDE AND PERSONNEL), LAISSEZ-FAIRE (MINDFUL AND RELAXED). REFLECT ON THIS AND WATCH HOW YOU CHANGE, WHAT TRIGGERS YOUR STYLE?

7: HOW MUCH ACTIVE LISTENING DID YOU DO? DID YOU LISTEN TO UNDERSTAND OR LISTEN TO REPLY? A KEY ERROR IS A COACH FORMULATING THE NEXT QUESTION INSTEAD OF LISTENING.

8: IF YOU USED NO TOOLS OR TECHNIQUES TODAY HOW DID THAT MAKE YOU FEEL? DID YOU LEAVE THINKING YOU MISSED SOMETHING? WHAT COULD YOU CHANGE FOR NEXT TIME?

9: WHAT PERCENTAGE OF THE SESSION WAS DRIVEN BY YOU? HOW MUCH OF THE SESSION WERE YOU RELAXED AND NOTICED WHAT CAME UP IN THE SESSION?

10: HOW MUCH OF THE SESSION WAS ABOUT YOU AND HOW MUCH ABOUT THE CLIENT? HOW COULD YOU LOOK AT THIS IN MORE DETAIL?

DATE:-   /   /

1: HOW MUCH GUIDING VS TELLING DID YOU DO? WHO WAS THIS FOR YOU OR THE CLIENT? WHAT COULD YOU DO DIFFERENTLY TO GROW?

2: WHAT MODELS HAVE YOU USED TODAY? BEHAVIOURAL MODELS OR NOTICING EMOTIONS AND FEELINGS? WHAT COULD YOU THINK ABOUT DIFFERENTLY FOR THE NEXT SESSION?

3: HOW MUCH OF YOUR WORK IS A HABIT? WHAT NEW HABITS WOULD YOU LIKE TO CREATE AND WHAT ONES WOULD YOU LIKE TO DELETE LIKE AN APP ON YOUR PHONE. THINK ABOUT ONE FOR YOUR NEXT SESSION.

4: HOW WAS YOUR CLIENT RELATIONSHIP TODAY, WHY WAS THIS? WHAT WOULD YOU LIKE TO BE DIFFERENT?

5: WHAT TOOLS HAVE YOU USED TODAY, WHY? DID YOU PREPARE TO USE THEM? IF THIS IS THE CASE WHAT MIGHT YOU HAVE MISSED BY NOT PAYING ATTENTION? WHAT COULD YOU DO DIFFERENTLY NEXT TIME?

6: WHAT WAS YOUR STYLE TODAY? AUTOCRATIC (BOSSY AND AUTHORITIVE) DEMOCRATIC (GUIDE AND PERSONNEL), LAISSEZ-FAIRE (MINDFUL AND RELAXED). REFLECT ON THIS AND WATCH HOW YOU CHANGE, WHAT TRIGGERS YOUR STYLE?

7: HOW MUCH ACTIVE LISTENING DID YOU DO? DID YOU LISTEN TO UNDERSTAND OR LISTEN TO REPLY? A KEY ERROR IS A COACH FORMULATING THE NEXT QUESTION INSTEAD OF LISTENING.

8: IF YOU USED NO TOOLS OR TECHNIQUES TODAY HOW DID THAT MAKE YOU FEEL? DID YOU LEAVE THINKING YOU MISSED SOMETHING? WHAT COULD YOU CHANGE FOR NEXT TIME?

9: WHAT PERCENTAGE OF THE SESSION WAS DRIVEN BY YOU? HOW MUCH OF THE SESSION WERE YOU RELAXED AND NOTICED WHAT CAME UP IN THE SESSION?

10: HOW MUCH OF THE SESSION WAS ABOUT YOU AND HOW MUCH ABOUT THE CLIENT? HOW COULD YOU LOOK AT THIS IN MORE DETAIL?

DATE:-   /   /

1: HOW MUCH GUIDING VS TELLING DID YOU DO? WHO WAS THIS FOR YOU OR THE CLIENT? WHAT COULD YOU DO DIFFERENTLY TO GROW?

2: WHAT MODELS HAVE YOU USED TODAY? BEHAVIOURAL MODELS OR NOTICING EMOTIONS AND FEELINGS? WHAT COULD YOU THINK ABOUT DIFFERENTLY FOR THE NEXT SESSION?

3: HOW MUCH OF YOUR WORK IS A HABIT? WHAT NEW HABITS WOULD YOU LIKE TO CREATE AND WHAT ONES WOULD YOU LIKE TO DELETE LIKE AN APP ON YOUR PHONE. THINK ABOUT ONE FOR YOUR NEXT SESSION.

4: HOW WAS YOUR CLIENT RELATIONSHIP TODAY, WHY WAS THIS? WHAT WOULD YOU LIKE TO BE DIFFERENT?

5: WHAT TOOLS HAVE YOU USED TODAY, WHY? DID YOU PREPARE TO USE THEM? IF THIS IS THE CASE WHAT MIGHT YOU HAVE MISSED BY NOT PAYING ATTENTION? WHAT COULD YOU DO DIFFERENTLY NEXT TIME?

6: WHAT WAS YOUR STYLE TODAY? AUTOCRATIC (BOSSY AND AUTHORITIVE) DEMOCRATIC (GUIDE AND PERSONNEL), LAISSEZ-FAIRE (MINDFUL AND RELAXED). REFLECT ON THIS AND WATCH HOW YOU CHANGE, WHAT TRIGGERS YOUR STYLE?

7: HOW MUCH ACTIVE LISTENING DID YOU DO? DID YOU LISTEN TO UNDERSTAND OR LISTEN TO REPLY? A KEY ERROR IS A COACH FORMULATING THE NEXT QUESTION INSTEAD OF LISTENING.

8: IF YOU USED NO TOOLS OR TECHNIQUES TODAY HOW DID THAT MAKE YOU FEEL? DID YOU LEAVE THINKING YOU MISSED SOMETHING? WHAT COULD YOU CHANGE FOR NEXT TIME?

9: WHAT PERCENTAGE OF THE SESSION WAS DRIVEN BY YOU? HOW MUCH OF THE SESSION WERE YOU RELAXED AND NOTICED WHAT CAME UP IN THE SESSION?

10: HOW MUCH OF THE SESSION WAS ABOUT YOU AND HOW MUCH ABOUT THE CLIENT? HOW COULD YOU LOOK AT THIS IN MORE DETAIL?

DATE:-   /   /

1: HOW MUCH GUIDING VS TELLING DID YOU DO? WHO WAS THIS FOR YOU OR THE CLIENT? WHAT COULD YOU DO DIFFERENTLY TO GROW?

2: WHAT MODELS HAVE YOU USED TODAY? BEHAVIOURAL MODELS OR NOTICING EMOTIONS AND FEELINGS? WHAT COULD YOU THINK ABOUT DIFFERENTLY FOR THE NEXT SESSION?

3: HOW MUCH OF YOUR WORK IS A HABIT? WHAT NEW HABITS WOULD YOU LIKE TO CREATE AND WHAT ONES WOULD YOU LIKE TO DELETE LIKE AN APP ON YOUR PHONE. THINK ABOUT ONE FOR YOUR NEXT SESSION.

4: HOW WAS YOUR CLIENT RELATIONSHIP TODAY, WHY WAS THIS? WHAT WOULD YOU LIKE TO BE DIFFERENT?

5: WHAT TOOLS HAVE YOU USED TODAY, WHY? DID YOU PREPARE TO USE THEM? IF THIS IS THE CASE WHAT MIGHT YOU HAVE MISSED BY NOT PAYING ATTENTION? WHAT COULD YOU DO DIFFERENTLY NEXT TIME?

6: WHAT WAS YOUR STYLE TODAY? AUTOCRATIC (BOSSY AND AUTHORITIVE) DEMOCRATIC (GUIDE AND PERSONNEL), LAISSEZ-FAIRE (MINDFUL AND RELAXED). REFLECT ON THIS AND WATCH HOW YOU CHANGE, WHAT TRIGGERS YOUR STYLE?

7: HOW MUCH ACTIVE LISTENING DID YOU DO? DID YOU LISTEN TO UNDERSTAND OR LISTEN TO REPLY? A KEY ERROR IS A COACH FORMULATING THE NEXT QUESTION INSTEAD OF LISTENING.

8: IF YOU USED NO TOOLS OR TECHNIQUES TODAY HOW DID THAT MAKE YOU FEEL? DID YOU LEAVE THINKING YOU MISSED SOMETHING? WHAT COULD YOU CHANGE FOR NEXT TIME?

9: WHAT PERCENTAGE OF THE SESSION WAS DRIVEN BY YOU? HOW MUCH OF THE SESSION WERE YOU RELAXED AND NOTICED WHAT CAME UP IN THE SESSION?

10: HOW MUCH OF THE SESSION WAS ABOUT YOU AND HOW MUCH ABOUT THE CLIENT? HOW COULD YOU LOOK AT THIS IN MORE DETAIL?

DATE:-   /   /

1: HOW MUCH GUIDING VS TELLING DID YOU DO? WHO WAS THIS FOR YOU OR THE CLIENT? WHAT COULD YOU DO DIFFERENTLY TO GROW?

2: WHAT MODELS HAVE YOU USED TODAY? BEHAVIOURAL MODELS OR NOTICING EMOTIONS AND FEELINGS? WHAT COULD YOU THINK ABOUT DIFFERENTLY FOR THE NEXT SESSION?

3: HOW MUCH OF YOUR WORK IS A HABIT? WHAT NEW HABITS WOULD YOU LIKE TO CREATE AND WHAT ONES WOULD YOU LIKE TO DELETE LIKE AN APP ON YOUR PHONE. THINK ABOUT ONE FOR YOUR NEXT SESSION.

4: HOW WAS YOUR CLIENT RELATIONSHIP TODAY, WHY WAS THIS? WHAT WOULD YOU LIKE TO BE DIFFERENT?

5: WHAT TOOLS HAVE YOU USED TODAY, WHY? DID YOU PREPARE TO USE THEM? IF THIS IS THE CASE WHAT MIGHT YOU HAVE MISSED BY NOT PAYING ATTENTION? WHAT COULD YOU DO DIFFERENTLY NEXT TIME?

6: WHAT WAS YOUR STYLE TODAY? AUTOCRATIC (BOSSY AND AUTHORITIVE) DEMOCRATIC (GUIDE AND PERSONNEL), LAISSEZ-FAIRE (MINDFUL AND RELAXED). REFLECT ON THIS AND WATCH HOW YOU CHANGE, WHAT TRIGGERS YOUR STYLE?

7: HOW MUCH ACTIVE LISTENING DID YOU DO? DID YOU LISTEN TO UNDERSTAND OR LISTEN TO REPLY? A KEY ERROR IS A COACH FORMULATING THE NEXT QUESTION INSTEAD OF LISTENING.

8: IF YOU USED NO TOOLS OR TECHNIQUES TODAY HOW DID THAT MAKE YOU FEEL? DID YOU LEAVE THINKING YOU MISSED SOMETHING? WHAT COULD YOU CHANGE FOR NEXT TIME?

9: WHAT PERCENTAGE OF THE SESSION WAS DRIVEN BY YOU? HOW MUCH OF THE SESSION WERE YOU RELAXED AND NOTICED WHAT CAME UP IN THE SESSION?

10: HOW MUCH OF THE SESSION WAS ABOUT YOU AND HOW MUCH ABOUT THE CLIENT? HOW COULD YOU LOOK AT THIS IN MORE DETAIL?

DATE:-   /   /

1: HOW MUCH GUIDING VS TELLING DID YOU DO? WHO WAS THIS FOR YOU OR THE CLIENT? WHAT COULD YOU DO DIFFERENTLY TO GROW?

2: WHAT MODELS HAVE YOU USED TODAY? BEHAVIOURAL MODELS OR NOTICING EMOTIONS AND FEELINGS? WHAT COULD YOU THINK ABOUT DIFFERENTLY FOR THE NEXT SESSION?

3: HOW MUCH OF YOUR WORK IS A HABIT? WHAT NEW HABITS WOULD YOU LIKE TO CREATE AND WHAT ONES WOULD YOU LIKE TO DELETE LIKE AN APP ON YOUR PHONE. THINK ABOUT ONE FOR YOUR NEXT SESSION.

4: HOW WAS YOUR CLIENT RELATIONSHIP TODAY, WHY WAS THIS? WHAT WOULD YOU LIKE TO BE DIFFERENT?

5: WHAT TOOLS HAVE YOU USED TODAY, WHY? DID YOU PREPARE TO USE THEM? IF THIS IS THE CASE WHAT MIGHT YOU HAVE MISSED BY NOT PAYING ATTENTION? WHAT COULD YOU DO DIFFERENTLY NEXT TIME?

6: WHAT WAS YOUR STYLE TODAY? AUTOCRATIC (BOSSY AND AUTHORITIVE) DEMOCRATIC (GUIDE AND PERSONNEL), LAISSEZ-FAIRE (MINDFUL AND RELAXED). REFLECT ON THIS AND WATCH HOW YOU CHANGE, WHAT TRIGGERS YOUR STYLE?

7: HOW MUCH ACTIVE LISTENING DID YOU DO? DID YOU LISTEN TO UNDERSTAND OR LISTEN TO REPLY? A KEY ERROR IS A COACH FORMULATING THE NEXT QUESTION INSTEAD OF LISTENING.

8: IF YOU USED NO TOOLS OR TECHNIQUES TODAY HOW DID THAT MAKE YOU FEEL? DID YOU LEAVE THINKING YOU MISSED SOMETHING? WHAT COULD YOU CHANGE FOR NEXT TIME?

9: WHAT PERCENTAGE OF THE SESSION WAS DRIVEN BY YOU? HOW MUCH OF THE SESSION WERE YOU RELAXED AND NOTICED WHAT CAME UP IN THE SESSION?

10: HOW MUCH OF THE SESSION WAS ABOUT YOU AND HOW MUCH ABOUT THE CLIENT? HOW COULD YOU LOOK AT THIS IN MORE DETAIL?

1: HOW HAVE I GROWN OVER THE LAST 10 DAYS

2: WHAT AM I GOING TO FOCUS ON OVER THE NEXT 10 DAYS?

3: WHAT FIVE THINGS AM I POSITIVELY TAKING FROM THE LAST 10 DAYS AND MOVING THEM FORWARD INTO THE NEXT 10 DAYS.

-
-
-
-
-

4: WHAT KEY AREAS WOULD I LIKE TO CONCENTRATE ON?

"What do you do with a mistake: recognize it, admit it, learn from it, forget it."

DEAN SMITH

DATE:-   /   /

1: HOW MUCH GUIDING VS TELLING DID YOU DO? WHO WAS THIS
FOR YOU OR THE CLIENT? WHAT COULD YOU DO DIFFERENTLY TO GROW?

2: WHAT MODELS HAVE YOU USED TODAY? BEHAVIOURAL MODELS OR
NOTICING EMOTIONS AND FEELINGS? WHAT COULD YOU THINK ABOUT
DIFFERENTLY FOR THE NEXT SESSION?

3: HOW MUCH OF YOUR WORK IS A HABIT? WHAT NEW HABITS WOULD
YOU LIKE TO CREATE AND WHAT ONES WOULD YOU LIKE TO DELETE LIKE
AN APP ON YOUR PHONE. THINK ABOUT ONE FOR YOUR NEXT SESSION.

4: HOW WAS YOUR CLIENT RELATIONSHIP TODAY, WHY WAS THIS?
WHAT WOULD YOU LIKE TO BE DIFFERENT?

5: WHAT TOOLS HAVE YOU USED TODAY, WHY? DID YOU PREPARE TO
USE THEM? IF THIS IS THE CASE WHAT MIGHT YOU HAVE MISSED BY NOT
PAYING ATTENTION? WHAT COULD YOU DO DIFFERENTLY NEXT TIME?

6: WHAT WAS YOUR STYLE TODAY? AUTOCRATIC (BOSSY AND AUTHORITIVE) DEMOCRATIC (GUIDE AND PERSONNEL), LAISSEZ-FAIRE (MINDFUL AND RELAXED). REFLECT ON THIS AND WATCH HOW YOU CHANGE, WHAT TRIGGERS YOUR STYLE?

7: HOW MUCH ACTIVE LISTENING DID YOU DO? DID YOU LISTEN TO UNDERSTAND OR LISTEN TO REPLY? A KEY ERROR IS A COACH FORMULATING THE NEXT QUESTION INSTEAD OF LISTENING.

8: IF YOU USED NO TOOLS OR TECHNIQUES TODAY HOW DID THAT MAKE YOU FEEL? DID YOU LEAVE THINKING YOU MISSED SOMETHING? WHAT COULD YOU CHANGE FOR NEXT TIME?

9: WHAT PERCENTAGE OF THE SESSION WAS DRIVEN BY YOU? HOW MUCH OF THE SESSION WERE YOU RELAXED AND NOTICED WHAT CAME UP IN THE SESSION?

10: HOW MUCH OF THE SESSION WAS ABOUT YOU AND HOW MUCH ABOUT THE CLIENT? HOW COULD YOU LOOK AT THIS IN MORE DETAIL?

DATE:-   /   /

1: HOW MUCH GUIDING VS TELLING DID YOU DO? WHO WAS THIS FOR YOU OR THE CLIENT? WHAT COULD YOU DO DIFFERENTLY TO GROW?

2: WHAT MODELS HAVE YOU USED TODAY? BEHAVIOURAL MODELS OR NOTICING EMOTIONS AND FEELINGS? WHAT COULD YOU THINK ABOUT DIFFERENTLY FOR THE NEXT SESSION?

3: HOW MUCH OF YOUR WORK IS A HABIT? WHAT NEW HABITS WOULD YOU LIKE TO CREATE AND WHAT ONES WOULD YOU LIKE TO DELETE LIKE AN APP ON YOUR PHONE. THINK ABOUT ONE FOR YOUR NEXT SESSION.

4: HOW WAS YOUR CLIENT RELATIONSHIP TODAY, WHY WAS THIS? WHAT WOULD YOU LIKE TO BE DIFFERENT?

5: WHAT TOOLS HAVE YOU USED TODAY, WHY? DID YOU PREPARE TO USE THEM? IF THIS IS THE CASE WHAT MIGHT YOU HAVE MISSED BY NOT PAYING ATTENTION? WHAT COULD YOU DO DIFFERENTLY NEXT TIME?

6: WHAT WAS YOUR STYLE TODAY? AUTOCRATIC (BOSSY AND AUTHORITIVE) DEMOCRATIC (GUIDE AND PERSONNEL), LAISSEZ-FAIRE (MINDFUL AND RELAXED). REFLECT ON THIS AND WATCH HOW YOU CHANGE, WHAT TRIGGERS YOUR STYLE?

7: HOW MUCH ACTIVE LISTENING DID YOU DO? DID YOU LISTEN TO UNDERSTAND OR LISTEN TO REPLY? A KEY ERROR IS A COACH FORMULATING THE NEXT QUESTION INSTEAD OF LISTENING.

8: IF YOU USED NO TOOLS OR TECHNIQUES TODAY HOW DID THAT MAKE YOU FEEL? DID YOU LEAVE THINKING YOU MISSED SOMETHING? WHAT COULD YOU CHANGE FOR NEXT TIME?

9: WHAT PERCENTAGE OF THE SESSION WAS DRIVEN BY YOU? HOW MUCH OF THE SESSION WERE YOU RELAXED AND NOTICED WHAT CAME UP IN THE SESSION?

10: HOW MUCH OF THE SESSION WAS ABOUT YOU AND HOW MUCH ABOUT THE CLIENT? HOW COULD YOU LOOK AT THIS IN MORE DETAIL?

DATE:-   /   /

1: HOW MUCH GUIDING VS TELLING DID YOU DO? WHO WAS THIS
FOR YOU OR THE CLIENT? WHAT COULD YOU DO DIFFERENTLY TO GROW?

2: WHAT MODELS HAVE YOU USED TODAY? BEHAVIOURAL MODELS OR
NOTICING EMOTIONS AND FEELINGS? WHAT COULD YOU THINK ABOUT
DIFFERENTLY FOR THE NEXT SESSION?

3: HOW MUCH OF YOUR WORK IS A HABIT? WHAT NEW HABITS WOULD
YOU LIKE TO CREATE AND WHAT ONES WOULD YOU LIKE TO DELETE LIKE
AN APP ON YOUR PHONE. THINK ABOUT ONE FOR YOUR NEXT SESSION.

4: HOW WAS YOUR CLIENT RELATIONSHIP TODAY, WHY WAS THIS?
WHAT WOULD YOU LIKE TO BE DIFFERENT?

5: WHAT TOOLS HAVE YOU USED TODAY, WHY? DID YOU PREPARE TO
USE THEM? IF THIS IS THE CASE WHAT MIGHT YOU HAVE MISSED BY NOT
PAYING ATTENTION? WHAT COULD YOU DO DIFFERENTLY NEXT TIME?

6: WHAT WAS YOUR STYLE TODAY? AUTOCRATIC (BOSSY AND AUTHORITIVE) DEMOCRATIC (GUIDE AND PERSONNEL), LAISSEZ-FAIRE (MINDFUL AND RELAXED). REFLECT ON THIS AND WATCH HOW YOU CHANGE, WHAT TRIGGERS YOUR STYLE?

7: HOW MUCH ACTIVE LISTENING DID YOU DO? DID YOU LISTEN TO UNDERSTAND OR LISTEN TO REPLY? A KEY ERROR IS A COACH FORMULATING THE NEXT QUESTION INSTEAD OF LISTENING.

8: IF YOU USED NO TOOLS OR TECHNIQUES TODAY HOW DID THAT MAKE YOU FEEL? DID YOU LEAVE THINKING YOU MISSED SOMETHING? WHAT COULD YOU CHANGE FOR NEXT TIME?

9: WHAT PERCENTAGE OF THE SESSION WAS DRIVEN BY YOU? HOW MUCH OF THE SESSION WERE YOU RELAXED AND NOTICED WHAT CAME UP IN THE SESSION?

10: HOW MUCH OF THE SESSION WAS ABOUT YOU AND HOW MUCH ABOUT THE CLIENT? HOW COULD YOU LOOK AT THIS IN MORE DETAIL?

DATE:-   /   /

1: HOW MUCH GUIDING VS TELLING DID YOU DO? WHO WAS THIS FOR YOU OR THE CLIENT? WHAT COULD YOU DO DIFFERENTLY TO GROW?

2: WHAT MODELS HAVE YOU USED TODAY? BEHAVIOURAL MODELS OR NOTICING EMOTIONS AND FEELINGS? WHAT COULD YOU THINK ABOUT DIFFERENTLY FOR THE NEXT SESSION?

3: HOW MUCH OF YOUR WORK IS A HABIT? WHAT NEW HABITS WOULD YOU LIKE TO CREATE AND WHAT ONES WOULD YOU LIKE TO DELETE LIKE AN APP ON YOUR PHONE. THINK ABOUT ONE FOR YOUR NEXT SESSION.

4: HOW WAS YOUR CLIENT RELATIONSHIP TODAY, WHY WAS THIS? WHAT WOULD YOU LIKE TO BE DIFFERENT?

5: WHAT TOOLS HAVE YOU USED TODAY, WHY? DID YOU PREPARE TO USE THEM? IF THIS IS THE CASE WHAT MIGHT YOU HAVE MISSED BY NOT PAYING ATTENTION? WHAT COULD YOU DO DIFFERENTLY NEXT TIME?

6: WHAT WAS YOUR STYLE TODAY? AUTOCRATIC (BOSSY AND AUTHORITIVE) DEMOCRATIC (GUIDE AND PERSONNEL), LAISSEZ-FAIRE (MINDFUL AND RELAXED). REFLECT ON THIS AND WATCH HOW YOU CHANGE, WHAT TRIGGERS YOUR STYLE?

7: HOW MUCH ACTIVE LISTENING DID YOU DO? DID YOU LISTEN TO UNDERSTAND OR LISTEN TO REPLY? A KEY ERROR IS A COACH FORMULATING THE NEXT QUESTION INSTEAD OF LISTENING.

8: IF YOU USED NO TOOLS OR TECHNIQUES TODAY HOW DID THAT MAKE YOU FEEL? DID YOU LEAVE THINKING YOU MISSED SOMETHING? WHAT COULD YOU CHANGE FOR NEXT TIME?

9: WHAT PERCENTAGE OF THE SESSION WAS DRIVEN BY YOU? HOW MUCH OF THE SESSION WERE YOU RELAXED AND NOTICED WHAT CAME UP IN THE SESSION?

10: HOW MUCH OF THE SESSION WAS ABOUT YOU AND HOW MUCH ABOUT THE CLIENT? HOW COULD YOU LOOK AT THIS IN MORE DETAIL?

DATE:-   /   /

1: HOW MUCH GUIDING VS TELLING DID YOU DO? WHO WAS THIS FOR YOU OR THE CLIENT? WHAT COULD YOU DO DIFFERENTLY TO GROW?

2: WHAT MODELS HAVE YOU USED TODAY? BEHAVIOURAL MODELS OR NOTICING EMOTIONS AND FEELINGS? WHAT COULD YOU THINK ABOUT DIFFERENTLY FOR THE NEXT SESSION?

3: HOW MUCH OF YOUR WORK IS A HABIT? WHAT NEW HABITS WOULD YOU LIKE TO CREATE AND WHAT ONES WOULD YOU LIKE TO DELETE LIKE AN APP ON YOUR PHONE. THINK ABOUT ONE FOR YOUR NEXT SESSION.

4: HOW WAS YOUR CLIENT RELATIONSHIP TODAY, WHY WAS THIS? WHAT WOULD YOU LIKE TO BE DIFFERENT?

5: WHAT TOOLS HAVE YOU USED TODAY, WHY? DID YOU PREPARE TO USE THEM? IF THIS IS THE CASE WHAT MIGHT YOU HAVE MISSED BY NOT PAYING ATTENTION? WHAT COULD YOU DO DIFFERENTLY NEXT TIME?

6: WHAT WAS YOUR STYLE TODAY? AUTOCRATIC (BOSSY AND AUTHORITIVE) DEMOCRATIC (GUIDE AND PERSONNEL), LAISSEZ-FAIRE (MINDFUL AND RELAXED). REFLECT ON THIS AND WATCH HOW YOU CHANGE, WHAT TRIGGERS YOUR STYLE?

7: HOW MUCH ACTIVE LISTENING DID YOU DO? DID YOU LISTEN TO UNDERSTAND OR LISTEN TO REPLY? A KEY ERROR IS A COACH FORMULATING THE NEXT QUESTION INSTEAD OF LISTENING.

8: IF YOU USED NO TOOLS OR TECHNIQUES TODAY HOW DID THAT MAKE YOU FEEL? DID YOU LEAVE THINKING YOU MISSED SOMETHING? WHAT COULD YOU CHANGE FOR NEXT TIME?

9: WHAT PERCENTAGE OF THE SESSION WAS DRIVEN BY YOU? HOW MUCH OF THE SESSION WERE YOU RELAXED AND NOTICED WHAT CAME UP IN THE SESSION?

10: HOW MUCH OF THE SESSION WAS ABOUT YOU AND HOW MUCH ABOUT THE CLIENT? HOW COULD YOU LOOK AT THIS IN MORE DETAIL?

DATE:-   /   /

1: HOW MUCH GUIDING VS TELLING DID YOU DO? WHO WAS THIS FOR YOU OR THE CLIENT? WHAT COULD YOU DO DIFFERENTLY TO GROW?

2: WHAT MODELS HAVE YOU USED TODAY? BEHAVIOURAL MODELS OR NOTICING EMOTIONS AND FEELINGS? WHAT COULD YOU THINK ABOUT DIFFERENTLY FOR THE NEXT SESSION?

3: HOW MUCH OF YOUR WORK IS A HABIT? WHAT NEW HABITS WOULD YOU LIKE TO CREATE AND WHAT ONES WOULD YOU LIKE TO DELETE LIKE AN APP ON YOUR PHONE. THINK ABOUT ONE FOR YOUR NEXT SESSION.

4: HOW WAS YOUR CLIENT RELATIONSHIP TODAY, WHY WAS THIS? WHAT WOULD YOU LIKE TO BE DIFFERENT?

5: WHAT TOOLS HAVE YOU USED TODAY, WHY? DID YOU PREPARE TO USE THEM? IF THIS IS THE CASE WHAT MIGHT YOU HAVE MISSED BY NOT PAYING ATTENTION? WHAT COULD YOU DO DIFFERENTLY NEXT TIME?

6: WHAT WAS YOUR STYLE TODAY? AUTOCRATIC (BOSSY AND AUTHORITIVE) DEMOCRATIC (GUIDE AND PERSONNEL), LAISSEZ-FAIRE (MINDFUL AND RELAXED). REFLECT ON THIS AND WATCH HOW YOU CHANGE, WHAT TRIGGERS YOUR STYLE?

7: HOW MUCH ACTIVE LISTENING DID YOU DO? DID YOU LISTEN TO UNDERSTAND OR LISTEN TO REPLY? A KEY ERROR IS A COACH FORMULATING THE NEXT QUESTION INSTEAD OF LISTENING.

8: IF YOU USED NO TOOLS OR TECHNIQUES TODAY HOW DID THAT MAKE YOU FEEL? DID YOU LEAVE THINKING YOU MISSED SOMETHING? WHAT COULD YOU CHANGE FOR NEXT TIME?

9: WHAT PERCENTAGE OF THE SESSION WAS DRIVEN BY YOU? HOW MUCH OF THE SESSION WERE YOU RELAXED AND NOTICED WHAT CAME UP IN THE SESSION?

10: HOW MUCH OF THE SESSION WAS ABOUT YOU AND HOW MUCH ABOUT THE CLIENT? HOW COULD YOU LOOK AT THIS IN MORE DETAIL?

DATE:-   /   /

1: HOW MUCH GUIDING VS TELLING DID YOU DO? WHO WAS THIS FOR YOU OR THE CLIENT? WHAT COULD YOU DO DIFFERENTLY TO GROW?

2: WHAT MODELS HAVE YOU USED TODAY? BEHAVIOURAL MODELS OR NOTICING EMOTIONS AND FEELINGS? WHAT COULD YOU THINK ABOUT DIFFERENTLY FOR THE NEXT SESSION?

3: HOW MUCH OF YOUR WORK IS A HABIT? WHAT NEW HABITS WOULD YOU LIKE TO CREATE AND WHAT ONES WOULD YOU LIKE TO DELETE LIKE AN APP ON YOUR PHONE. THINK ABOUT ONE FOR YOUR NEXT SESSION.

4: HOW WAS YOUR CLIENT RELATIONSHIP TODAY, WHY WAS THIS? WHAT WOULD YOU LIKE TO BE DIFFERENT?

5: WHAT TOOLS HAVE YOU USED TODAY, WHY? DID YOU PREPARE TO USE THEM? IF THIS IS THE CASE WHAT MIGHT YOU HAVE MISSED BY NOT PAYING ATTENTION? WHAT COULD YOU DO DIFFERENTLY NEXT TIME?

6: WHAT WAS YOUR STYLE TODAY? AUTOCRATIC (BOSSY AND AUTHORITIVE) DEMOCRATIC (GUIDE AND PERSONNEL), LAISSEZ-FAIRE (MINDFUL AND RELAXED). REFLECT ON THIS AND WATCH HOW YOU CHANGE, WHAT TRIGGERS YOUR STYLE?

7: HOW MUCH ACTIVE LISTENING DID YOU DO? DID YOU LISTEN TO UNDERSTAND OR LISTEN TO REPLY? A KEY ERROR IS A COACH FORMULATING THE NEXT QUESTION INSTEAD OF LISTENING.

8: IF YOU USED NO TOOLS OR TECHNIQUES TODAY HOW DID THAT MAKE YOU FEEL? DID YOU LEAVE THINKING YOU MISSED SOMETHING? WHAT COULD YOU CHANGE FOR NEXT TIME?

9: WHAT PERCENTAGE OF THE SESSION WAS DRIVEN BY YOU? HOW MUCH OF THE SESSION WERE YOU RELAXED AND NOTICED WHAT CAME UP IN THE SESSION?

10: HOW MUCH OF THE SESSION WAS ABOUT YOU AND HOW MUCH ABOUT THE CLIENT? HOW COULD YOU LOOK AT THIS IN MORE DETAIL?

DATE:-   /   /

1: HOW MUCH GUIDING VS TELLING DID YOU DO? WHO WAS THIS FOR YOU OR THE CLIENT? WHAT COULD YOU DO DIFFERENTLY TO GROW?

2: WHAT MODELS HAVE YOU USED TODAY? BEHAVIOURAL MODELS OR NOTICING EMOTIONS AND FEELINGS? WHAT COULD YOU THINK ABOUT DIFFERENTLY FOR THE NEXT SESSION?

3: HOW MUCH OF YOUR WORK IS A HABIT? WHAT NEW HABITS WOULD YOU LIKE TO CREATE AND WHAT ONES WOULD YOU LIKE TO DELETE LIKE AN APP ON YOUR PHONE. THINK ABOUT ONE FOR YOUR NEXT SESSION.

4: HOW WAS YOUR CLIENT RELATIONSHIP TODAY, WHY WAS THIS? WHAT WOULD YOU LIKE TO BE DIFFERENT?

5: WHAT TOOLS HAVE YOU USED TODAY, WHY? DID YOU PREPARE TO USE THEM? IF THIS IS THE CASE WHAT MIGHT YOU HAVE MISSED BY NOT PAYING ATTENTION? WHAT COULD YOU DO DIFFERENTLY NEXT TIME?

6: WHAT WAS YOUR STYLE TODAY? AUTOCRATIC (BOSSY AND AUTHORITIVE) DEMOCRATIC (GUIDE AND PERSONNEL), LAISSEZ-FAIRE (MINDFUL AND RELAXED). REFLECT ON THIS AND WATCH HOW YOU CHANGE, WHAT TRIGGERS YOUR STYLE?

7: HOW MUCH ACTIVE LISTENING DID YOU DO? DID YOU LISTEN TO UNDERSTAND OR LISTEN TO REPLY? A KEY ERROR IS A COACH FORMULATING THE NEXT QUESTION INSTEAD OF LISTENING.

8: IF YOU USED NO TOOLS OR TECHNIQUES TODAY HOW DID THAT MAKE YOU FEEL? DID YOU LEAVE THINKING YOU MISSED SOMETHING? WHAT COULD YOU CHANGE FOR NEXT TIME?

9: WHAT PERCENTAGE OF THE SESSION WAS DRIVEN BY YOU? HOW MUCH OF THE SESSION WERE YOU RELAXED AND NOTICED WHAT CAME UP IN THE SESSION?

10: HOW MUCH OF THE SESSION WAS ABOUT YOU AND HOW MUCH ABOUT THE CLIENT? HOW COULD YOU LOOK AT THIS IN MORE DETAIL?

DATE:-   /   /

1: HOW MUCH GUIDING VS TELLING DID YOU DO? WHO WAS THIS FOR YOU OR THE CLIENT? WHAT COULD YOU DO DIFFERENTLY TO GROW?

2: WHAT MODELS HAVE YOU USED TODAY? BEHAVIOURAL MODELS OR NOTICING EMOTIONS AND FEELINGS? WHAT COULD YOU THINK ABOUT DIFFERENTLY FOR THE NEXT SESSION?

3: HOW MUCH OF YOUR WORK IS A HABIT? WHAT NEW HABITS WOULD YOU LIKE TO CREATE AND WHAT ONES WOULD YOU LIKE TO DELETE LIKE AN APP ON YOUR PHONE. THINK ABOUT ONE FOR YOUR NEXT SESSION.

4: HOW WAS YOUR CLIENT RELATIONSHIP TODAY, WHY WAS THIS? WHAT WOULD YOU LIKE TO BE DIFFERENT?

5: WHAT TOOLS HAVE YOU USED TODAY, WHY? DID YOU PREPARE TO USE THEM? IF THIS IS THE CASE WHAT MIGHT YOU HAVE MISSED BY NOT PAYING ATTENTION? WHAT COULD YOU DO DIFFERENTLY NEXT TIME?

6: WHAT WAS YOUR STYLE TODAY? AUTOCRATIC (BOSSY AND AUTHORITIVE) DEMOCRATIC (GUIDE AND PERSONNEL), LAISSEZ-FAIRE (MINDFUL AND RELAXED). REFLECT ON THIS AND WATCH HOW YOU CHANGE, WHAT TRIGGERS YOUR STYLE?

7: HOW MUCH ACTIVE LISTENING DID YOU DO? DID YOU LISTEN TO UNDERSTAND OR LISTEN TO REPLY? A KEY ERROR IS A COACH FORMULATING THE NEXT QUESTION INSTEAD OF LISTENING.

8: IF YOU USED NO TOOLS OR TECHNIQUES TODAY HOW DID THAT MAKE YOU FEEL? DID YOU LEAVE THINKING YOU MISSED SOMETHING? WHAT COULD YOU CHANGE FOR NEXT TIME?

9: WHAT PERCENTAGE OF THE SESSION WAS DRIVEN BY YOU? HOW MUCH OF THE SESSION WERE YOU RELAXED AND NOTICED WHAT CAME UP IN THE SESSION?

10: HOW MUCH OF THE SESSION WAS ABOUT YOU AND HOW MUCH ABOUT THE CLIENT? HOW COULD YOU LOOK AT THIS IN MORE DETAIL?

REFLECTION ON YOUR USE OF TOOLS AND TECHNIQUES IN COACHING

DATE:-   /   /

1: HOW MUCH GUIDING VS TELLING DID YOU DO? WHO WAS THIS FOR YOU OR THE CLIENT? WHAT COULD YOU DO DIFFERENTLY TO GROW?

2: WHAT MODELS HAVE YOU USED TODAY? BEHAVIOURAL MODELS OR NOTICING EMOTIONS AND FEELINGS? WHAT COULD YOU THINK ABOUT DIFFERENTLY FOR THE NEXT SESSION?

3: HOW MUCH OF YOUR WORK IS A HABIT? WHAT NEW HABITS WOULD YOU LIKE TO CREATE AND WHAT ONES WOULD YOU LIKE TO DELETE LIKE AN APP ON YOUR PHONE. THINK ABOUT ONE FOR YOUR NEXT SESSION.

4: HOW WAS YOUR CLIENT RELATIONSHIP TODAY, WHY WAS THIS? WHAT WOULD YOU LIKE TO BE DIFFERENT?

5: WHAT TOOLS HAVE YOU USED TODAY, WHY? DID YOU PREPARE TO USE THEM? IF THIS IS THE CASE WHAT MIGHT YOU HAVE MISSED BY NOT PAYING ATTENTION? WHAT COULD YOU DO DIFFERENTLY NEXT TIME?

6: WHAT WAS YOUR STYLE TODAY? AUTOCRATIC (BOSSY AND AUTHORITIVE) DEMOCRATIC (GUIDE AND PERSONNEL), LAISSEZ-FAIRE (MINDFUL AND RELAXED). REFLECT ON THIS AND WATCH HOW YOU CHANGE, WHAT TRIGGERS YOUR STYLE?

7: HOW MUCH ACTIVE LISTENING DID YOU DO? DID YOU LISTEN TO UNDERSTAND OR LISTEN TO REPLY? A KEY ERROR IS A COACH FORMULATING THE NEXT QUESTION INSTEAD OF LISTENING.

8: IF YOU USED NO TOOLS OR TECHNIQUES TODAY HOW DID THAT MAKE YOU FEEL? DID YOU LEAVE THINKING YOU MISSED SOMETHING? WHAT COULD YOU CHANGE FOR NEXT TIME?

9: WHAT PERCENTAGE OF THE SESSION WAS DRIVEN BY YOU? HOW MUCH OF THE SESSION WERE YOU RELAXED AND NOTICED WHAT CAME UP IN THE SESSION?

10: HOW MUCH OF THE SESSION WAS ABOUT YOU AND HOW MUCH ABOUT THE CLIENT? HOW COULD YOU LOOK AT THIS IN MORE DETAIL?

1: HOW HAVE I GROWN OVER THE LAST 10 DAYS

2: WHAT AM I GOING TO FOCUS ON OVER THE NEXT 10 DAYS?

3: WHAT FIVE THINGS AM I POSITIVELY TAKING FROM THE LAST 10 DAYS AND MOVING THEM FORWARD INTO THE NEXT 10 DAYS.

-
-
-
-
-

4: WHAT KEY AREAS WOULD I LIKE TO CONCENTRATE ON?

"In basketball — as in life — true joy comes from being fully present in each and every moment, not just when things are going your way."

PHIL JACKSON

DATE:-   /   /

1: HOW MUCH GUIDING VS TELLING DID YOU DO? WHO WAS THIS FOR YOU OR THE CLIENT? WHAT COULD YOU DO DIFFERENTLY TO GROW?

2: WHAT MODELS HAVE YOU USED TODAY? BEHAVIOURAL MODELS OR NOTICING EMOTIONS AND FEELINGS? WHAT COULD YOU THINK ABOUT DIFFERENTLY FOR THE NEXT SESSION?

3: HOW MUCH OF YOUR WORK IS A HABIT? WHAT NEW HABITS WOULD YOU LIKE TO CREATE AND WHAT ONES WOULD YOU LIKE TO DELETE LIKE AN APP ON YOUR PHONE. THINK ABOUT ONE FOR YOUR NEXT SESSION.

4: HOW WAS YOUR CLIENT RELATIONSHIP TODAY, WHY WAS THIS? WHAT WOULD YOU LIKE TO BE DIFFERENT?

5: WHAT TOOLS HAVE YOU USED TODAY, WHY? DID YOU PREPARE TO USE THEM? IF THIS IS THE CASE WHAT MIGHT YOU HAVE MISSED BY NOT PAYING ATTENTION? WHAT COULD YOU DO DIFFERENTLY NEXT TIME?

6: WHAT WAS YOUR STYLE TODAY? AUTOCRATIC (BOSSY AND AUTHORITIVE) DEMOCRATIC (GUIDE AND PERSONNEL), LAISSEZ-FAIRE (MINDFUL AND RELAXED). REFLECT ON THIS AND WATCH HOW YOU CHANGE, WHAT TRIGGERS YOUR STYLE?

7: HOW MUCH ACTIVE LISTENING DID YOU DO? DID YOU LISTEN TO UNDERSTAND OR LISTEN TO REPLY? A KEY ERROR IS A COACH FORMULATING THE NEXT QUESTION INSTEAD OF LISTENING.

8: IF YOU USED NO TOOLS OR TECHNIQUES TODAY HOW DID THAT MAKE YOU FEEL? DID YOU LEAVE THINKING YOU MISSED SOMETHING? WHAT COULD YOU CHANGE FOR NEXT TIME?

9: WHAT PERCENTAGE OF THE SESSION WAS DRIVEN BY YOU? HOW MUCH OF THE SESSION WERE YOU RELAXED AND NOTICED WHAT CAME UP IN THE SESSION?

10: HOW MUCH OF THE SESSION WAS ABOUT YOU AND HOW MUCH ABOUT THE CLIENT? HOW COULD YOU LOOK AT THIS IN MORE DETAIL?

DATE:-   /   /

1: HOW MUCH GUIDING VS TELLING DID YOU DO? WHO WAS THIS FOR YOU OR THE CLIENT? WHAT COULD YOU DO DIFFERENTLY TO GROW?

2: WHAT MODELS HAVE YOU USED TODAY? BEHAVIOURAL MODELS OR NOTICING EMOTIONS AND FEELINGS? WHAT COULD YOU THINK ABOUT DIFFERENTLY FOR THE NEXT SESSION?

3: HOW MUCH OF YOUR WORK IS A HABIT? WHAT NEW HABITS WOULD YOU LIKE TO CREATE AND WHAT ONES WOULD YOU LIKE TO DELETE LIKE AN APP ON YOUR PHONE. THINK ABOUT ONE FOR YOUR NEXT SESSION.

4: HOW WAS YOUR CLIENT RELATIONSHIP TODAY, WHY WAS THIS? WHAT WOULD YOU LIKE TO BE DIFFERENT?

5: WHAT TOOLS HAVE YOU USED TODAY, WHY? DID YOU PREPARE TO USE THEM? IF THIS IS THE CASE WHAT MIGHT YOU HAVE MISSED BY NOT PAYING ATTENTION? WHAT COULD YOU DO DIFFERENTLY NEXT TIME?

6: WHAT WAS YOUR STYLE TODAY? AUTOCRATIC (BOSSY AND AUTHORITIVE) DEMOCRATIC (GUIDE AND PERSONNEL), LAISSEZ-FAIRE (MINDFUL AND RELAXED). REFLECT ON THIS AND WATCH HOW YOU CHANGE, WHAT TRIGGERS YOUR STYLE?

7: HOW MUCH ACTIVE LISTENING DID YOU DO? DID YOU LISTEN TO UNDERSTAND OR LISTEN TO REPLY? A KEY ERROR IS A COACH FORMULATING THE NEXT QUESTION INSTEAD OF LISTENING.

8: IF YOU USED NO TOOLS OR TECHNIQUES TODAY HOW DID THAT MAKE YOU FEEL? DID YOU LEAVE THINKING YOU MISSED SOMETHING? WHAT COULD YOU CHANGE FOR NEXT TIME?

9: WHAT PERCENTAGE OF THE SESSION WAS DRIVEN BY YOU? HOW MUCH OF THE SESSION WERE YOU RELAXED AND NOTICED WHAT CAME UP IN THE SESSION?

10: HOW MUCH OF THE SESSION WAS ABOUT YOU AND HOW MUCH ABOUT THE CLIENT? HOW COULD YOU LOOK AT THIS IN MORE DETAIL?

DATE:-   /   /

1: HOW MUCH GUIDING VS TELLING DID YOU DO? WHO WAS THIS FOR YOU OR THE CLIENT? WHAT COULD YOU DO DIFFERENTLY TO GROW?

2: WHAT MODELS HAVE YOU USED TODAY? BEHAVIOURAL MODELS OR NOTICING EMOTIONS AND FEELINGS? WHAT COULD YOU THINK ABOUT DIFFERENTLY FOR THE NEXT SESSION?

3: HOW MUCH OF YOUR WORK IS A HABIT? WHAT NEW HABITS WOULD YOU LIKE TO CREATE AND WHAT ONES WOULD YOU LIKE TO DELETE LIKE AN APP ON YOUR PHONE. THINK ABOUT ONE FOR YOUR NEXT SESSION.

4: HOW WAS YOUR CLIENT RELATIONSHIP TODAY, WHY WAS THIS? WHAT WOULD YOU LIKE TO BE DIFFERENT?

5: WHAT TOOLS HAVE YOU USED TODAY, WHY? DID YOU PREPARE TO USE THEM? IF THIS IS THE CASE WHAT MIGHT YOU HAVE MISSED BY NOT PAYING ATTENTION? WHAT COULD YOU DO DIFFERENTLY NEXT TIME?

6: WHAT WAS YOUR STYLE TODAY? AUTOCRATIC (BOSSY AND AUTHORITIVE) DEMOCRATIC (GUIDE AND PERSONNEL), LAISSEZ-FAIRE (MINDFUL AND RELAXED). REFLECT ON THIS AND WATCH HOW YOU CHANGE, WHAT TRIGGERS YOUR STYLE?

7: HOW MUCH ACTIVE LISTENING DID YOU DO? DID YOU LISTEN TO UNDERSTAND OR LISTEN TO REPLY? A KEY ERROR IS A COACH FORMULATING THE NEXT QUESTION INSTEAD OF LISTENING.

8: IF YOU USED NO TOOLS OR TECHNIQUES TODAY HOW DID THAT MAKE YOU FEEL? DID YOU LEAVE THINKING YOU MISSED SOMETHING? WHAT COULD YOU CHANGE FOR NEXT TIME?

9: WHAT PERCENTAGE OF THE SESSION WAS DRIVEN BY YOU? HOW MUCH OF THE SESSION WERE YOU RELAXED AND NOTICED WHAT CAME UP IN THE SESSION?

10: HOW MUCH OF THE SESSION WAS ABOUT YOU AND HOW MUCH ABOUT THE CLIENT? HOW COULD YOU LOOK AT THIS IN MORE DETAIL?

DATE:-   /   /

1: HOW MUCH GUIDING VS TELLING DID YOU DO? WHO WAS THIS FOR YOU OR THE CLIENT? WHAT COULD YOU DO DIFFERENTLY TO GROW?

2: WHAT MODELS HAVE YOU USED TODAY? BEHAVIOURAL MODELS OR NOTICING EMOTIONS AND FEELINGS? WHAT COULD YOU THINK ABOUT DIFFERENTLY FOR THE NEXT SESSION?

3: HOW MUCH OF YOUR WORK IS A HABIT? WHAT NEW HABITS WOULD YOU LIKE TO CREATE AND WHAT ONES WOULD YOU LIKE TO DELETE LIKE AN APP ON YOUR PHONE. THINK ABOUT ONE FOR YOUR NEXT SESSION.

4: HOW WAS YOUR CLIENT RELATIONSHIP TODAY, WHY WAS THIS? WHAT WOULD YOU LIKE TO BE DIFFERENT?

5: WHAT TOOLS HAVE YOU USED TODAY, WHY? DID YOU PREPARE TO USE THEM? IF THIS IS THE CASE WHAT MIGHT YOU HAVE MISSED BY NOT PAYING ATTENTION? WHAT COULD YOU DO DIFFERENTLY NEXT TIME?

6: WHAT WAS YOUR STYLE TODAY? AUTOCRATIC (BOSSY AND AUTHORITIVE) DEMOCRATIC (GUIDE AND PERSONNEL), LAISSEZ-FAIRE (MINDFUL AND RELAXED). REFLECT ON THIS AND WATCH HOW YOU CHANGE, WHAT TRIGGERS YOUR STYLE?

7: HOW MUCH ACTIVE LISTENING DID YOU DO? DID YOU LISTEN TO UNDERSTAND OR LISTEN TO REPLY? A KEY ERROR IS A COACH FORMULATING THE NEXT QUESTION INSTEAD OF LISTENING.

8: IF YOU USED NO TOOLS OR TECHNIQUES TODAY HOW DID THAT MAKE YOU FEEL? DID YOU LEAVE THINKING YOU MISSED SOMETHING? WHAT COULD YOU CHANGE FOR NEXT TIME?

9: WHAT PERCENTAGE OF THE SESSION WAS DRIVEN BY YOU? HOW MUCH OF THE SESSION WERE YOU RELAXED AND NOTICED WHAT CAME UP IN THE SESSION?

10: HOW MUCH OF THE SESSION WAS ABOUT YOU AND HOW MUCH ABOUT THE CLIENT? HOW COULD YOU LOOK AT THIS IN MORE DETAIL?

DATE:-   /   /

1: HOW MUCH GUIDING VS TELLING DID YOU DO? WHO WAS THIS FOR YOU OR THE CLIENT? WHAT COULD YOU DO DIFFERENTLY TO GROW?

2: WHAT MODELS HAVE YOU USED TODAY? BEHAVIOURAL MODELS OR NOTICING EMOTIONS AND FEELINGS? WHAT COULD YOU THINK ABOUT DIFFERENTLY FOR THE NEXT SESSION?

3: HOW MUCH OF YOUR WORK IS A HABIT? WHAT NEW HABITS WOULD YOU LIKE TO CREATE AND WHAT ONES WOULD YOU LIKE TO DELETE LIKE AN APP ON YOUR PHONE. THINK ABOUT ONE FOR YOUR NEXT SESSION.

4: HOW WAS YOUR CLIENT RELATIONSHIP TODAY, WHY WAS THIS? WHAT WOULD YOU LIKE TO BE DIFFERENT?

5: WHAT TOOLS HAVE YOU USED TODAY, WHY? DID YOU PREPARE TO USE THEM? IF THIS IS THE CASE WHAT MIGHT YOU HAVE MISSED BY NOT PAYING ATTENTION? WHAT COULD YOU DO DIFFERENTLY NEXT TIME?

6: WHAT WAS YOUR STYLE TODAY? AUTOCRATIC (BOSSY AND
AUTHORITIVE) DEMOCRATIC (GUIDE AND PERSONNEL), LAISSEZ-FAIRE
(MINDFUL AND RELAXED). REFLECT ON THIS AND WATCH HOW YOU
CHANGE, WHAT TRIGGERS YOUR STYLE?

7: HOW MUCH ACTIVE LISTENING DID YOU DO? DID YOU LISTEN
TO UNDERSTAND OR LISTEN TO REPLY? A KEY ERROR IS A COACH
FORMULATING THE NEXT QUESTION INSTEAD OF LISTENING.

8: IF YOU USED NO TOOLS OR TECHNIQUES TODAY HOW DID
THAT MAKE YOU FEEL? DID YOU LEAVE THINKING YOU MISSED
SOMETHING? WHAT COULD YOU CHANGE FOR NEXT TIME?

9: WHAT PERCENTAGE OF THE SESSION WAS DRIVEN BY YOU?
HOW MUCH OF THE SESSION WERE YOU RELAXED AND NOTICED WHAT
CAME UP IN THE SESSION?

10: HOW MUCH OF THE SESSION WAS ABOUT YOU AND HOW MUCH
ABOUT THE CLIENT? HOW COULD YOU LOOK AT THIS IN MORE DETAIL?

DATE:-   /   /

1: HOW MUCH GUIDING VS TELLING DID YOU DO? WHO WAS THIS
FOR YOU OR THE CLIENT? WHAT COULD YOU DO DIFFERENTLY TO GROW?

2: WHAT MODELS HAVE YOU USED TODAY? BEHAVIOURAL MODELS OR
NOTICING EMOTIONS AND FEELINGS? WHAT COULD YOU THINK ABOUT
DIFFERENTLY FOR THE NEXT SESSION?

3: HOW MUCH OF YOUR WORK IS A HABIT? WHAT NEW HABITS WOULD
YOU LIKE TO CREATE AND WHAT ONES WOULD YOU LIKE TO DELETE LIKE
AN APP ON YOUR PHONE. THINK ABOUT ONE FOR YOUR NEXT SESSION.

4: HOW WAS YOUR CLIENT RELATIONSHIP TODAY, WHY WAS THIS?
WHAT WOULD YOU LIKE TO BE DIFFERENT?

5: WHAT TOOLS HAVE YOU USED TODAY, WHY? DID YOU PREPARE TO
USE THEM? IF THIS IS THE CASE WHAT MIGHT YOU HAVE MISSED BY NOT
PAYING ATTENTION? WHAT COULD YOU DO DIFFERENTLY NEXT TIME?

6: WHAT WAS YOUR STYLE TODAY? AUTOCRATIC (BOSSY AND AUTHORITIVE) DEMOCRATIC (GUIDE AND PERSONNEL), LAISSEZ-FAIRE (MINDFUL AND RELAXED). REFLECT ON THIS AND WATCH HOW YOU CHANGE, WHAT TRIGGERS YOUR STYLE?

7: HOW MUCH ACTIVE LISTENING DID YOU DO? DID YOU LISTEN TO UNDERSTAND OR LISTEN TO REPLY? A KEY ERROR IS A COACH FORMULATING THE NEXT QUESTION INSTEAD OF LISTENING.

8: IF YOU USED NO TOOLS OR TECHNIQUES TODAY HOW DID THAT MAKE YOU FEEL? DID YOU LEAVE THINKING YOU MISSED SOMETHING? WHAT COULD YOU CHANGE FOR NEXT TIME?

9: WHAT PERCENTAGE OF THE SESSION WAS DRIVEN BY YOU? HOW MUCH OF THE SESSION WERE YOU RELAXED AND NOTICED WHAT CAME UP IN THE SESSION?

10: HOW MUCH OF THE SESSION WAS ABOUT YOU AND HOW MUCH ABOUT THE CLIENT? HOW COULD YOU LOOK AT THIS IN MORE DETAIL?

DATE:-   /   /

1: HOW MUCH GUIDING VS TELLING DID YOU DO? WHO WAS THIS FOR YOU OR THE CLIENT? WHAT COULD YOU DO DIFFERENTLY TO GROW?

2: WHAT MODELS HAVE YOU USED TODAY? BEHAVIOURAL MODELS OR NOTICING EMOTIONS AND FEELINGS? WHAT COULD YOU THINK ABOUT DIFFERENTLY FOR THE NEXT SESSION?

3: HOW MUCH OF YOUR WORK IS A HABIT? WHAT NEW HABITS WOULD YOU LIKE TO CREATE AND WHAT ONES WOULD YOU LIKE TO DELETE LIKE AN APP ON YOUR PHONE. THINK ABOUT ONE FOR YOUR NEXT SESSION.

4: HOW WAS YOUR CLIENT RELATIONSHIP TODAY, WHY WAS THIS? WHAT WOULD YOU LIKE TO BE DIFFERENT?

5: WHAT TOOLS HAVE YOU USED TODAY, WHY? DID YOU PREPARE TO USE THEM? IF THIS IS THE CASE WHAT MIGHT YOU HAVE MISSED BY NOT PAYING ATTENTION? WHAT COULD YOU DO DIFFERENTLY NEXT TIME?

6: WHAT WAS YOUR STYLE TODAY? AUTOCRATIC (BOSSY AND AUTHORITIVE) DEMOCRATIC (GUIDE AND PERSONNEL), LAISSEZ-FAIRE (MINDFUL AND RELAXED). REFLECT ON THIS AND WATCH HOW YOU CHANGE, WHAT TRIGGERS YOUR STYLE?

7: HOW MUCH ACTIVE LISTENING DID YOU DO? DID YOU LISTEN TO UNDERSTAND OR LISTEN TO REPLY? A KEY ERROR IS A COACH FORMULATING THE NEXT QUESTION INSTEAD OF LISTENING.

8: IF YOU USED NO TOOLS OR TECHNIQUES TODAY HOW DID THAT MAKE YOU FEEL? DID YOU LEAVE THINKING YOU MISSED SOMETHING? WHAT COULD YOU CHANGE FOR NEXT TIME?

9: WHAT PERCENTAGE OF THE SESSION WAS DRIVEN BY YOU? HOW MUCH OF THE SESSION WERE YOU RELAXED AND NOTICED WHAT CAME UP IN THE SESSION?

10: HOW MUCH OF THE SESSION WAS ABOUT YOU AND HOW MUCH ABOUT THE CLIENT? HOW COULD YOU LOOK AT THIS IN MORE DETAIL?

DATE:-   /   /

1: HOW MUCH GUIDING VS TELLING DID YOU DO? WHO WAS THIS FOR YOU OR THE CLIENT? WHAT COULD YOU DO DIFFERENTLY TO GROW?

2: WHAT MODELS HAVE YOU USED TODAY? BEHAVIOURAL MODELS OR NOTICING EMOTIONS AND FEELINGS? WHAT COULD YOU THINK ABOUT DIFFERENTLY FOR THE NEXT SESSION?

3: HOW MUCH OF YOUR WORK IS A HABIT? WHAT NEW HABITS WOULD YOU LIKE TO CREATE AND WHAT ONES WOULD YOU LIKE TO DELETE LIKE AN APP ON YOUR PHONE. THINK ABOUT ONE FOR YOUR NEXT SESSION.

4: HOW WAS YOUR CLIENT RELATIONSHIP TODAY, WHY WAS THIS? WHAT WOULD YOU LIKE TO BE DIFFERENT?

5: WHAT TOOLS HAVE YOU USED TODAY, WHY? DID YOU PREPARE TO USE THEM? IF THIS IS THE CASE WHAT MIGHT YOU HAVE MISSED BY NOT PAYING ATTENTION? WHAT COULD YOU DO DIFFERENTLY NEXT TIME?

6: WHAT WAS YOUR STYLE TODAY? AUTOCRATIC (BOSSY AND AUTHORITIVE) DEMOCRATIC (GUIDE AND PERSONNEL), LAISSEZ-FAIRE (MINDFUL AND RELAXED). REFLECT ON THIS AND WATCH HOW YOU CHANGE, WHAT TRIGGERS YOUR STYLE?

7: HOW MUCH ACTIVE LISTENING DID YOU DO? DID YOU LISTEN TO UNDERSTAND OR LISTEN TO REPLY? A KEY ERROR IS A COACH FORMULATING THE NEXT QUESTION INSTEAD OF LISTENING.

8: IF YOU USED NO TOOLS OR TECHNIQUES TODAY HOW DID THAT MAKE YOU FEEL? DID YOU LEAVE THINKING YOU MISSED SOMETHING? WHAT COULD YOU CHANGE FOR NEXT TIME?

9: WHAT PERCENTAGE OF THE SESSION WAS DRIVEN BY YOU? HOW MUCH OF THE SESSION WERE YOU RELAXED AND NOTICED WHAT CAME UP IN THE SESSION?

10: HOW MUCH OF THE SESSION WAS ABOUT YOU AND HOW MUCH ABOUT THE CLIENT? HOW COULD YOU LOOK AT THIS IN MORE DETAIL?

DATE:-   /   /

1: HOW MUCH GUIDING VS TELLING DID YOU DO? WHO WAS THIS
FOR YOU OR THE CLIENT? WHAT COULD YOU DO DIFFERENTLY TO GROW?

2: WHAT MODELS HAVE YOU USED TODAY? BEHAVIOURAL MODELS OR
NOTICING EMOTIONS AND FEELINGS? WHAT COULD YOU THINK ABOUT
DIFFERENTLY FOR THE NEXT SESSION?

3: HOW MUCH OF YOUR WORK IS A HABIT? WHAT NEW HABITS WOULD
YOU LIKE TO CREATE AND WHAT ONES WOULD YOU LIKE TO DELETE LIKE
AN APP ON YOUR PHONE. THINK ABOUT ONE FOR YOUR NEXT SESSION.

4: HOW WAS YOUR CLIENT RELATIONSHIP TODAY, WHY WAS THIS?
WHAT WOULD YOU LIKE TO BE DIFFERENT?

5: WHAT TOOLS HAVE YOU USED TODAY, WHY? DID YOU PREPARE TO
USE THEM? IF THIS IS THE CASE WHAT MIGHT YOU HAVE MISSED BY NOT
PAYING ATTENTION? WHAT COULD YOU DO DIFFERENTLY NEXT TIME?

6: WHAT WAS YOUR STYLE TODAY? AUTOCRATIC (BOSSY AND AUTHORITIVE) DEMOCRATIC (GUIDE AND PERSONNEL), LAISSEZ-FAIRE (MINDFUL AND RELAXED). REFLECT ON THIS AND WATCH HOW YOU CHANGE, WHAT TRIGGERS YOUR STYLE?

7: HOW MUCH ACTIVE LISTENING DID YOU DO? DID YOU LISTEN TO UNDERSTAND OR LISTEN TO REPLY? A KEY ERROR IS A COACH FORMULATING THE NEXT QUESTION INSTEAD OF LISTENING.

8: IF YOU USED NO TOOLS OR TECHNIQUES TODAY HOW DID THAT MAKE YOU FEEL? DID YOU LEAVE THINKING YOU MISSED SOMETHING? WHAT COULD YOU CHANGE FOR NEXT TIME?

9: WHAT PERCENTAGE OF THE SESSION WAS DRIVEN BY YOU? HOW MUCH OF THE SESSION WERE YOU RELAXED AND NOTICED WHAT CAME UP IN THE SESSION?

10: HOW MUCH OF THE SESSION WAS ABOUT YOU AND HOW MUCH ABOUT THE CLIENT? HOW COULD YOU LOOK AT THIS IN MORE DETAIL?

DATE:-   /   /

1: HOW MUCH GUIDING VS TELLING DID YOU DO? WHO WAS THIS FOR YOU OR THE CLIENT? WHAT COULD YOU DO DIFFERENTLY TO GROW?

2: WHAT MODELS HAVE YOU USED TODAY? BEHAVIOURAL MODELS OR NOTICING EMOTIONS AND FEELINGS? WHAT COULD YOU THINK ABOUT DIFFERENTLY FOR THE NEXT SESSION?

3: HOW MUCH OF YOUR WORK IS A HABIT? WHAT NEW HABITS WOULD YOU LIKE TO CREATE AND WHAT ONES WOULD YOU LIKE TO DELETE LIKE AN APP ON YOUR PHONE. THINK ABOUT ONE FOR YOUR NEXT SESSION.

4: HOW WAS YOUR CLIENT RELATIONSHIP TODAY, WHY WAS THIS? WHAT WOULD YOU LIKE TO BE DIFFERENT?

5: WHAT TOOLS HAVE YOU USED TODAY, WHY? DID YOU PREPARE TO USE THEM? IF THIS IS THE CASE WHAT MIGHT YOU HAVE MISSED BY NOT PAYING ATTENTION? WHAT COULD YOU DO DIFFERENTLY NEXT TIME?

6: WHAT WAS YOUR STYLE TODAY? AUTOCRATIC (BOSSY AND AUTHORITIVE) DEMOCRATIC (GUIDE AND PERSONNEL), LAISSEZ-FAIRE (MINDFUL AND RELAXED). REFLECT ON THIS AND WATCH HOW YOU CHANGE, WHAT TRIGGERS YOUR STYLE?

7: HOW MUCH ACTIVE LISTENING DID YOU DO? DID YOU LISTEN TO UNDERSTAND OR LISTEN TO REPLY? A KEY ERROR IS A COACH FORMULATING THE NEXT QUESTION INSTEAD OF LISTENING.

8: IF YOU USED NO TOOLS OR TECHNIQUES TODAY HOW DID THAT MAKE YOU FEEL? DID YOU LEAVE THINKING YOU MISSED SOMETHING? WHAT COULD YOU CHANGE FOR NEXT TIME?

9: WHAT PERCENTAGE OF THE SESSION WAS DRIVEN BY YOU? HOW MUCH OF THE SESSION WERE YOU RELAXED AND NOTICED WHAT CAME UP IN THE SESSION?

10: HOW MUCH OF THE SESSION WAS ABOUT YOU AND HOW MUCH ABOUT THE CLIENT? HOW COULD YOU LOOK AT THIS IN MORE DETAIL?

REFLECTION ON YOUR USE OF TOOLS AND TECHNIQUES IN COACHING

1: HOW HAVE I GROWN OVER THE LAST 10 DAYS

2: WHAT AM I GOING TO FOCUS ON OVER THE NEXT 10 DAYS?

3: WHAT FIVE THINGS AM I POSITIVELY TAKING FROM THE LAST 10 DAYS AND MOVING THEM FORWARD INTO THE NEXT 10 DAYS.

-
-
-
-
-

4: WHAT KEY AREAS WOULD I LIKE TO CONCENTRATE ON?

Day 50
Congratulations

Congratulations for meeting the halfway point, tremendous effort and fantastic that you are reflecting effectively. The book is for you only, very personnel and as you reflect on the last fifty days, look at your incredible journey. Every little change is the change you need to move forward. Think about achieving your goal of improving and what will it feel like at day 100, just imagine that feeling.

DATE:-   /   /

1: HOW MUCH GUIDING VS TELLING DID YOU DO? WHO WAS THIS FOR YOU OR THE CLIENT? WHAT COULD YOU DO DIFFERENTLY TO GROW?

2: WHAT MODELS HAVE YOU USED TODAY? BEHAVIOURAL MODELS OR NOTICING EMOTIONS AND FEELINGS? WHAT COULD YOU THINK ABOUT DIFFERENTLY FOR THE NEXT SESSION?

3: HOW MUCH OF YOUR WORK IS A HABIT? WHAT NEW HABITS WOULD YOU LIKE TO CREATE AND WHAT ONES WOULD YOU LIKE TO DELETE LIKE AN APP ON YOUR PHONE. THINK ABOUT ONE FOR YOUR NEXT SESSION.

4: HOW WAS YOUR CLIENT RELATIONSHIP TODAY, WHY WAS THIS? WHAT WOULD YOU LIKE TO BE DIFFERENT?

5: WHAT TOOLS HAVE YOU USED TODAY, WHY? DID YOU PREPARE TO USE THEM? IF THIS IS THE CASE WHAT MIGHT YOU HAVE MISSED BY NOT PAYING ATTENTION? WHAT COULD YOU DO DIFFERENTLY NEXT TIME?

6: WHAT WAS YOUR STYLE TODAY? AUTOCRATIC (BOSSY AND AUTHORITIVE) DEMOCRATIC (GUIDE AND PERSONNEL), LAISSEZ-FAIRE (MINDFUL AND RELAXED). REFLECT ON THIS AND WATCH HOW YOU CHANGE, WHAT TRIGGERS YOUR STYLE?

7: HOW MUCH ACTIVE LISTENING DID YOU DO? DID YOU LISTEN TO UNDERSTAND OR LISTEN TO REPLY? A KEY ERROR IS A COACH FORMULATING THE NEXT QUESTION INSTEAD OF LISTENING.

8: IF YOU USED NO TOOLS OR TECHNIQUES TODAY HOW DID THAT MAKE YOU FEEL? DID YOU LEAVE THINKING YOU MISSED SOMETHING? WHAT COULD YOU CHANGE FOR NEXT TIME?

9: WHAT PERCENTAGE OF THE SESSION WAS DRIVEN BY YOU? HOW MUCH OF THE SESSION WERE YOU RELAXED AND NOTICED WHAT CAME UP IN THE SESSION?

10: HOW MUCH OF THE SESSION WAS ABOUT YOU AND HOW MUCH ABOUT THE CLIENT? HOW COULD YOU LOOK AT THIS IN MORE DETAIL?

DATE:-   /   /

1: HOW MUCH GUIDING VS TELLING DID YOU DO? WHO WAS THIS FOR YOU OR THE CLIENT? WHAT COULD YOU DO DIFFERENTLY TO GROW?

2: WHAT MODELS HAVE YOU USED TODAY? BEHAVIOURAL MODELS OR NOTICING EMOTIONS AND FEELINGS? WHAT COULD YOU THINK ABOUT DIFFERENTLY FOR THE NEXT SESSION?

3: HOW MUCH OF YOUR WORK IS A HABIT? WHAT NEW HABITS WOULD YOU LIKE TO CREATE AND WHAT ONES WOULD YOU LIKE TO DELETE LIKE AN APP ON YOUR PHONE. THINK ABOUT ONE FOR YOUR NEXT SESSION.

4: HOW WAS YOUR CLIENT RELATIONSHIP TODAY, WHY WAS THIS? WHAT WOULD YOU LIKE TO BE DIFFERENT?

5: WHAT TOOLS HAVE YOU USED TODAY, WHY? DID YOU PREPARE TO USE THEM? IF THIS IS THE CASE WHAT MIGHT YOU HAVE MISSED BY NOT PAYING ATTENTION? WHAT COULD YOU DO DIFFERENTLY NEXT TIME?

6: WHAT WAS YOUR STYLE TODAY? AUTOCRATIC (BOSSY AND AUTHORITIVE) DEMOCRATIC (GUIDE AND PERSONNEL), LAISSEZ-FAIRE (MINDFUL AND RELAXED). REFLECT ON THIS AND WATCH HOW YOU CHANGE, WHAT TRIGGERS YOUR STYLE?

7: HOW MUCH ACTIVE LISTENING DID YOU DO? DID YOU LISTEN TO UNDERSTAND OR LISTEN TO REPLY? A KEY ERROR IS A COACH FORMULATING THE NEXT QUESTION INSTEAD OF LISTENING.

8: IF YOU USED NO TOOLS OR TECHNIQUES TODAY HOW DID THAT MAKE YOU FEEL? DID YOU LEAVE THINKING YOU MISSED SOMETHING? WHAT COULD YOU CHANGE FOR NEXT TIME?

9: WHAT PERCENTAGE OF THE SESSION WAS DRIVEN BY YOU? HOW MUCH OF THE SESSION WERE YOU RELAXED AND NOTICED WHAT CAME UP IN THE SESSION?

10: HOW MUCH OF THE SESSION WAS ABOUT YOU AND HOW MUCH ABOUT THE CLIENT? HOW COULD YOU LOOK AT THIS IN MORE DETAIL?

DATE:-   /   /

1: HOW MUCH GUIDING VS TELLING DID YOU DO? WHO WAS THIS
FOR YOU OR THE CLIENT? WHAT COULD YOU DO DIFFERENTLY TO GROW?

2: WHAT MODELS HAVE YOU USED TODAY? BEHAVIOURAL MODELS OR
NOTICING EMOTIONS AND FEELINGS? WHAT COULD YOU THINK ABOUT
DIFFERENTLY FOR THE NEXT SESSION?

3: HOW MUCH OF YOUR WORK IS A HABIT? WHAT NEW HABITS WOULD
YOU LIKE TO CREATE AND WHAT ONES WOULD YOU LIKE TO DELETE LIKE
AN APP ON YOUR PHONE. THINK ABOUT ONE FOR YOUR NEXT SESSION.

4: HOW WAS YOUR CLIENT RELATIONSHIP TODAY, WHY WAS THIS?
WHAT WOULD YOU LIKE TO BE DIFFERENT?

5: WHAT TOOLS HAVE YOU USED TODAY, WHY? DID YOU PREPARE TO
USE THEM? IF THIS IS THE CASE WHAT MIGHT YOU HAVE MISSED BY NOT
PAYING ATTENTION? WHAT COULD YOU DO DIFFERENTLY NEXT TIME?

6: WHAT WAS YOUR STYLE TODAY? AUTOCRATIC (BOSSY AND AUTHORITIVE) DEMOCRATIC (GUIDE AND PERSONNEL), LAISSEZ-FAIRE (MINDFUL AND RELAXED). REFLECT ON THIS AND WATCH HOW YOU CHANGE, WHAT TRIGGERS YOUR STYLE?

7: HOW MUCH ACTIVE LISTENING DID YOU DO? DID YOU LISTEN TO UNDERSTAND OR LISTEN TO REPLY? A KEY ERROR IS A COACH FORMULATING THE NEXT QUESTION INSTEAD OF LISTENING.

8: IF YOU USED NO TOOLS OR TECHNIQUES TODAY HOW DID THAT MAKE YOU FEEL? DID YOU LEAVE THINKING YOU MISSED SOMETHING? WHAT COULD YOU CHANGE FOR NEXT TIME?

9: WHAT PERCENTAGE OF THE SESSION WAS DRIVEN BY YOU? HOW MUCH OF THE SESSION WERE YOU RELAXED AND NOTICED WHAT CAME UP IN THE SESSION?

10: HOW MUCH OF THE SESSION WAS ABOUT YOU AND HOW MUCH ABOUT THE CLIENT? HOW COULD YOU LOOK AT THIS IN MORE DETAIL?

DATE:-   /   /

1: HOW MUCH GUIDING VS TELLING DID YOU DO? WHO WAS THIS FOR YOU OR THE CLIENT? WHAT COULD YOU DO DIFFERENTLY TO GROW?

2: WHAT MODELS HAVE YOU USED TODAY? BEHAVIOURAL MODELS OR NOTICING EMOTIONS AND FEELINGS? WHAT COULD YOU THINK ABOUT DIFFERENTLY FOR THE NEXT SESSION?

3: HOW MUCH OF YOUR WORK IS A HABIT? WHAT NEW HABITS WOULD YOU LIKE TO CREATE AND WHAT ONES WOULD YOU LIKE TO DELETE LIKE AN APP ON YOUR PHONE. THINK ABOUT ONE FOR YOUR NEXT SESSION.

4: HOW WAS YOUR CLIENT RELATIONSHIP TODAY, WHY WAS THIS? WHAT WOULD YOU LIKE TO BE DIFFERENT?

5: WHAT TOOLS HAVE YOU USED TODAY, WHY? DID YOU PREPARE TO USE THEM? IF THIS IS THE CASE WHAT MIGHT YOU HAVE MISSED BY NOT PAYING ATTENTION? WHAT COULD YOU DO DIFFERENTLY NEXT TIME?

6: WHAT WAS YOUR STYLE TODAY? AUTOCRATIC (BOSSY AND AUTHORITIVE) DEMOCRATIC (GUIDE AND PERSONNEL), LAISSEZ-FAIRE (MINDFUL AND RELAXED). REFLECT ON THIS AND WATCH HOW YOU CHANGE, WHAT TRIGGERS YOUR STYLE?

7: HOW MUCH ACTIVE LISTENING DID YOU DO? DID YOU LISTEN TO UNDERSTAND OR LISTEN TO REPLY? A KEY ERROR IS A COACH FORMULATING THE NEXT QUESTION INSTEAD OF LISTENING.

8: IF YOU USED NO TOOLS OR TECHNIQUES TODAY HOW DID THAT MAKE YOU FEEL? DID YOU LEAVE THINKING YOU MISSED SOMETHING? WHAT COULD YOU CHANGE FOR NEXT TIME?

9: WHAT PERCENTAGE OF THE SESSION WAS DRIVEN BY YOU? HOW MUCH OF THE SESSION WERE YOU RELAXED AND NOTICED WHAT CAME UP IN THE SESSION?

10: HOW MUCH OF THE SESSION WAS ABOUT YOU AND HOW MUCH ABOUT THE CLIENT? HOW COULD YOU LOOK AT THIS IN MORE DETAIL?

DATE:-   /   /

1: HOW MUCH GUIDING VS TELLING DID YOU DO? WHO WAS THIS FOR YOU OR THE CLIENT? WHAT COULD YOU DO DIFFERENTLY TO GROW?

2: WHAT MODELS HAVE YOU USED TODAY? BEHAVIOURAL MODELS OR NOTICING EMOTIONS AND FEELINGS? WHAT COULD YOU THINK ABOUT DIFFERENTLY FOR THE NEXT SESSION?

3: HOW MUCH OF YOUR WORK IS A HABIT? WHAT NEW HABITS WOULD YOU LIKE TO CREATE AND WHAT ONES WOULD YOU LIKE TO DELETE LIKE AN APP ON YOUR PHONE. THINK ABOUT ONE FOR YOUR NEXT SESSION.

4: HOW WAS YOUR CLIENT RELATIONSHIP TODAY, WHY WAS THIS? WHAT WOULD YOU LIKE TO BE DIFFERENT?

5: WHAT TOOLS HAVE YOU USED TODAY, WHY? DID YOU PREPARE TO USE THEM? IF THIS IS THE CASE WHAT MIGHT YOU HAVE MISSED BY NOT PAYING ATTENTION? WHAT COULD YOU DO DIFFERENTLY NEXT TIME?

6: WHAT WAS YOUR STYLE TODAY? AUTOCRATIC (BOSSY AND AUTHORITIVE) DEMOCRATIC (GUIDE AND PERSONNEL), LAISSEZ-FAIRE (MINDFUL AND RELAXED). REFLECT ON THIS AND WATCH HOW YOU CHANGE, WHAT TRIGGERS YOUR STYLE?

7: HOW MUCH ACTIVE LISTENING DID YOU DO? DID YOU LISTEN TO UNDERSTAND OR LISTEN TO REPLY? A KEY ERROR IS A COACH FORMULATING THE NEXT QUESTION INSTEAD OF LISTENING.

8: IF YOU USED NO TOOLS OR TECHNIQUES TODAY HOW DID THAT MAKE YOU FEEL? DID YOU LEAVE THINKING YOU MISSED SOMETHING? WHAT COULD YOU CHANGE FOR NEXT TIME?

9: WHAT PERCENTAGE OF THE SESSION WAS DRIVEN BY YOU? HOW MUCH OF THE SESSION WERE YOU RELAXED AND NOTICED WHAT CAME UP IN THE SESSION?

10: HOW MUCH OF THE SESSION WAS ABOUT YOU AND HOW MUCH ABOUT THE CLIENT? HOW COULD YOU LOOK AT THIS IN MORE DETAIL?

DATE:-   /   /

1: HOW MUCH GUIDING VS TELLING DID YOU DO? WHO WAS THIS FOR YOU OR THE CLIENT? WHAT COULD YOU DO DIFFERENTLY TO GROW?

2: WHAT MODELS HAVE YOU USED TODAY? BEHAVIOURAL MODELS OR NOTICING EMOTIONS AND FEELINGS? WHAT COULD YOU THINK ABOUT DIFFERENTLY FOR THE NEXT SESSION?

3: HOW MUCH OF YOUR WORK IS A HABIT? WHAT NEW HABITS WOULD YOU LIKE TO CREATE AND WHAT ONES WOULD YOU LIKE TO DELETE LIKE AN APP ON YOUR PHONE. THINK ABOUT ONE FOR YOUR NEXT SESSION.

4: HOW WAS YOUR CLIENT RELATIONSHIP TODAY, WHY WAS THIS? WHAT WOULD YOU LIKE TO BE DIFFERENT?

5: WHAT TOOLS HAVE YOU USED TODAY, WHY? DID YOU PREPARE TO USE THEM? IF THIS IS THE CASE WHAT MIGHT YOU HAVE MISSED BY NOT PAYING ATTENTION? WHAT COULD YOU DO DIFFERENTLY NEXT TIME?

6: WHAT WAS YOUR STYLE TODAY? AUTOCRATIC (BOSSY AND AUTHORITIVE) DEMOCRATIC (GUIDE AND PERSONNEL), LAISSEZ-FAIRE (MINDFUL AND RELAXED). REFLECT ON THIS AND WATCH HOW YOU CHANGE, WHAT TRIGGERS YOUR STYLE?

7: HOW MUCH ACTIVE LISTENING DID YOU DO? DID YOU LISTEN TO UNDERSTAND OR LISTEN TO REPLY? A KEY ERROR IS A COACH FORMULATING THE NEXT QUESTION INSTEAD OF LISTENING.

8: IF YOU USED NO TOOLS OR TECHNIQUES TODAY HOW DID THAT MAKE YOU FEEL? DID YOU LEAVE THINKING YOU MISSED SOMETHING? WHAT COULD YOU CHANGE FOR NEXT TIME?

9: WHAT PERCENTAGE OF THE SESSION WAS DRIVEN BY YOU? HOW MUCH OF THE SESSION WERE YOU RELAXED AND NOTICED WHAT CAME UP IN THE SESSION?

10: HOW MUCH OF THE SESSION WAS ABOUT YOU AND HOW MUCH ABOUT THE CLIENT? HOW COULD YOU LOOK AT THIS IN MORE DETAIL?

DATE:-   /   /

1: HOW MUCH GUIDING VS TELLING DID YOU DO? WHO WAS THIS FOR YOU OR THE CLIENT? WHAT COULD YOU DO DIFFERENTLY TO GROW?

2: WHAT MODELS HAVE YOU USED TODAY? BEHAVIOURAL MODELS OR NOTICING EMOTIONS AND FEELINGS? WHAT COULD YOU THINK ABOUT DIFFERENTLY FOR THE NEXT SESSION?

3: HOW MUCH OF YOUR WORK IS A HABIT? WHAT NEW HABITS WOULD YOU LIKE TO CREATE AND WHAT ONES WOULD YOU LIKE TO DELETE LIKE AN APP ON YOUR PHONE. THINK ABOUT ONE FOR YOUR NEXT SESSION.

4: HOW WAS YOUR CLIENT RELATIONSHIP TODAY, WHY WAS THIS? WHAT WOULD YOU LIKE TO BE DIFFERENT?

5: WHAT TOOLS HAVE YOU USED TODAY, WHY? DID YOU PREPARE TO USE THEM? IF THIS IS THE CASE WHAT MIGHT YOU HAVE MISSED BY NOT PAYING ATTENTION? WHAT COULD YOU DO DIFFERENTLY NEXT TIME?

6: WHAT WAS YOUR STYLE TODAY? AUTOCRATIC (BOSSY AND AUTHORITIVE) DEMOCRATIC (GUIDE AND PERSONNEL), LAISSEZ-FAIRE (MINDFUL AND RELAXED). REFLECT ON THIS AND WATCH HOW YOU CHANGE, WHAT TRIGGERS YOUR STYLE?

7: HOW MUCH ACTIVE LISTENING DID YOU DO? DID YOU LISTEN TO UNDERSTAND OR LISTEN TO REPLY? A KEY ERROR IS A COACH FORMULATING THE NEXT QUESTION INSTEAD OF LISTENING.

8: IF YOU USED NO TOOLS OR TECHNIQUES TODAY HOW DID THAT MAKE YOU FEEL? DID YOU LEAVE THINKING YOU MISSED SOMETHING? WHAT COULD YOU CHANGE FOR NEXT TIME?

9: WHAT PERCENTAGE OF THE SESSION WAS DRIVEN BY YOU? HOW MUCH OF THE SESSION WERE YOU RELAXED AND NOTICED WHAT CAME UP IN THE SESSION?

10: HOW MUCH OF THE SESSION WAS ABOUT YOU AND HOW MUCH ABOUT THE CLIENT? HOW COULD YOU LOOK AT THIS IN MORE DETAIL?

DATE:-   /   /

1: HOW MUCH GUIDING VS TELLING DID YOU DO? WHO WAS THIS FOR YOU OR THE CLIENT? WHAT COULD YOU DO DIFFERENTLY TO GROW?

2: WHAT MODELS HAVE YOU USED TODAY? BEHAVIOURAL MODELS OR NOTICING EMOTIONS AND FEELINGS? WHAT COULD YOU THINK ABOUT DIFFERENTLY FOR THE NEXT SESSION?

3: HOW MUCH OF YOUR WORK IS A HABIT? WHAT NEW HABITS WOULD YOU LIKE TO CREATE AND WHAT ONES WOULD YOU LIKE TO DELETE LIKE AN APP ON YOUR PHONE. THINK ABOUT ONE FOR YOUR NEXT SESSION.

4: HOW WAS YOUR CLIENT RELATIONSHIP TODAY, WHY WAS THIS? WHAT WOULD YOU LIKE TO BE DIFFERENT?

5: WHAT TOOLS HAVE YOU USED TODAY, WHY? DID YOU PREPARE TO USE THEM? IF THIS IS THE CASE WHAT MIGHT YOU HAVE MISSED BY NOT PAYING ATTENTION? WHAT COULD YOU DO DIFFERENTLY NEXT TIME?

6: WHAT WAS YOUR STYLE TODAY? AUTOCRATIC (BOSSY AND AUTHORITIVE) DEMOCRATIC (GUIDE AND PERSONNEL), LAISSEZ-FAIRE (MINDFUL AND RELAXED). REFLECT ON THIS AND WATCH HOW YOU CHANGE, WHAT TRIGGERS YOUR STYLE?

7: HOW MUCH ACTIVE LISTENING DID YOU DO? DID YOU LISTEN TO UNDERSTAND OR LISTEN TO REPLY? A KEY ERROR IS A COACH FORMULATING THE NEXT QUESTION INSTEAD OF LISTENING.

8: IF YOU USED NO TOOLS OR TECHNIQUES TODAY HOW DID THAT MAKE YOU FEEL? DID YOU LEAVE THINKING YOU MISSED SOMETHING? WHAT COULD YOU CHANGE FOR NEXT TIME?

9: WHAT PERCENTAGE OF THE SESSION WAS DRIVEN BY YOU? HOW MUCH OF THE SESSION WERE YOU RELAXED AND NOTICED WHAT CAME UP IN THE SESSION?

10: HOW MUCH OF THE SESSION WAS ABOUT YOU AND HOW MUCH ABOUT THE CLIENT? HOW COULD YOU LOOK AT THIS IN MORE DETAIL?

DATE:-   /   /

1: HOW MUCH GUIDING VS TELLING DID YOU DO? WHO WAS THIS FOR YOU OR THE CLIENT? WHAT COULD YOU DO DIFFERENTLY TO GROW?

2: WHAT MODELS HAVE YOU USED TODAY? BEHAVIOURAL MODELS OR NOTICING EMOTIONS AND FEELINGS? WHAT COULD YOU THINK ABOUT DIFFERENTLY FOR THE NEXT SESSION?

3: HOW MUCH OF YOUR WORK IS A HABIT? WHAT NEW HABITS WOULD YOU LIKE TO CREATE AND WHAT ONES WOULD YOU LIKE TO DELETE LIKE AN APP ON YOUR PHONE. THINK ABOUT ONE FOR YOUR NEXT SESSION.

4: HOW WAS YOUR CLIENT RELATIONSHIP TODAY, WHY WAS THIS? WHAT WOULD YOU LIKE TO BE DIFFERENT?

5: WHAT TOOLS HAVE YOU USED TODAY, WHY? DID YOU PREPARE TO USE THEM? IF THIS IS THE CASE WHAT MIGHT YOU HAVE MISSED BY NOT PAYING ATTENTION? WHAT COULD YOU DO DIFFERENTLY NEXT TIME?

6: WHAT WAS YOUR STYLE TODAY? AUTOCRATIC (BOSSY AND AUTHORITIVE) DEMOCRATIC (GUIDE AND PERSONNEL), LAISSEZ-FAIRE (MINDFUL AND RELAXED). REFLECT ON THIS AND WATCH HOW YOU CHANGE, WHAT TRIGGERS YOUR STYLE?

7: HOW MUCH ACTIVE LISTENING DID YOU DO? DID YOU LISTEN TO UNDERSTAND OR LISTEN TO REPLY? A KEY ERROR IS A COACH FORMULATING THE NEXT QUESTION INSTEAD OF LISTENING.

8: IF YOU USED NO TOOLS OR TECHNIQUES TODAY HOW DID THAT MAKE YOU FEEL? DID YOU LEAVE THINKING YOU MISSED SOMETHING? WHAT COULD YOU CHANGE FOR NEXT TIME?

9: WHAT PERCENTAGE OF THE SESSION WAS DRIVEN BY YOU? HOW MUCH OF THE SESSION WERE YOU RELAXED AND NOTICED WHAT CAME UP IN THE SESSION?

10: HOW MUCH OF THE SESSION WAS ABOUT YOU AND HOW MUCH ABOUT THE CLIENT? HOW COULD YOU LOOK AT THIS IN MORE DETAIL?

DATE:-   /   /

1: HOW MUCH GUIDING VS TELLING DID YOU DO? WHO WAS THIS
FOR YOU OR THE CLIENT? WHAT COULD YOU DO DIFFERENTLY TO GROW?

2: WHAT MODELS HAVE YOU USED TODAY? BEHAVIOURAL MODELS OR
NOTICING EMOTIONS AND FEELINGS? WHAT COULD YOU THINK ABOUT
DIFFERENTLY FOR THE NEXT SESSION?

3: HOW MUCH OF YOUR WORK IS A HABIT? WHAT NEW HABITS WOULD
YOU LIKE TO CREATE AND WHAT ONES WOULD YOU LIKE TO DELETE LIKE
AN APP ON YOUR PHONE. THINK ABOUT ONE FOR YOUR NEXT SESSION.

4: HOW WAS YOUR CLIENT RELATIONSHIP TODAY, WHY WAS THIS?
WHAT WOULD YOU LIKE TO BE DIFFERENT?

5: WHAT TOOLS HAVE YOU USED TODAY, WHY? DID YOU PREPARE TO
USE THEM? IF THIS IS THE CASE WHAT MIGHT YOU HAVE MISSED BY NOT
PAYING ATTENTION? WHAT COULD YOU DO DIFFERENTLY NEXT TIME?

6: WHAT WAS YOUR STYLE TODAY? AUTOCRATIC (BOSSY AND AUTHORITIVE) DEMOCRATIC (GUIDE AND PERSONNEL), LAISSEZ-FAIRE (MINDFUL AND RELAXED). REFLECT ON THIS AND WATCH HOW YOU CHANGE, WHAT TRIGGERS YOUR STYLE?

7: HOW MUCH ACTIVE LISTENING DID YOU DO? DID YOU LISTEN TO UNDERSTAND OR LISTEN TO REPLY? A KEY ERROR IS A COACH FORMULATING THE NEXT QUESTION INSTEAD OF LISTENING.

8: IF YOU USED NO TOOLS OR TECHNIQUES TODAY HOW DID THAT MAKE YOU FEEL? DID YOU LEAVE THINKING YOU MISSED SOMETHING? WHAT COULD YOU CHANGE FOR NEXT TIME?

9: WHAT PERCENTAGE OF THE SESSION WAS DRIVEN BY YOU? HOW MUCH OF THE SESSION WERE YOU RELAXED AND NOTICED WHAT CAME UP IN THE SESSION?

10: HOW MUCH OF THE SESSION WAS ABOUT YOU AND HOW MUCH ABOUT THE CLIENT? HOW COULD YOU LOOK AT THIS IN MORE DETAIL?

REFLECTION ON YOUR USE OF TOOLS AND TECHNIQUES IN COACHING

1: HOW HAVE I GROWN OVER THE LAST 10 DAYS

2: WHAT AM I GOING TO FOCUS ON OVER THE NEXT 10 DAYS?

3: WHAT FIVE THINGS AM I POSITIVELY TAKING FROM THE LAST 10 DAYS AND MOVING THEM FORWARD INTO THE NEXT 10 DAYS.

-
-
-
-
-

4: WHAT KEY AREAS WOULD I LIKE TO CONCENTRATE ON?

"champions behave like champions before they are champions."

BILL WALSH

DATE:-   /   /

1: HOW MUCH GUIDING VS TELLING DID YOU DO? WHO WAS THIS FOR YOU OR THE CLIENT? WHAT COULD YOU DO DIFFERENTLY TO GROW?

2: WHAT MODELS HAVE YOU USED TODAY? BEHAVIOURAL MODELS OR NOTICING EMOTIONS AND FEELINGS? WHAT COULD YOU THINK ABOUT DIFFERENTLY FOR THE NEXT SESSION?

3: HOW MUCH OF YOUR WORK IS A HABIT? WHAT NEW HABITS WOULD YOU LIKE TO CREATE AND WHAT ONES WOULD YOU LIKE TO DELETE LIKE AN APP ON YOUR PHONE. THINK ABOUT ONE FOR YOUR NEXT SESSION.

4: HOW WAS YOUR CLIENT RELATIONSHIP TODAY, WHY WAS THIS? WHAT WOULD YOU LIKE TO BE DIFFERENT?

5: WHAT TOOLS HAVE YOU USED TODAY, WHY? DID YOU PREPARE TO USE THEM? IF THIS IS THE CASE WHAT MIGHT YOU HAVE MISSED BY NOT PAYING ATTENTION? WHAT COULD YOU DO DIFFERENTLY NEXT TIME?

6: WHAT WAS YOUR STYLE TODAY? AUTOCRATIC (BOSSY AND AUTHORITIVE) DEMOCRATIC (GUIDE AND PERSONNEL), LAISSEZ-FAIRE (MINDFUL AND RELAXED). REFLECT ON THIS AND WATCH HOW YOU CHANGE, WHAT TRIGGERS YOUR STYLE?

7: HOW MUCH ACTIVE LISTENING DID YOU DO? DID YOU LISTEN TO UNDERSTAND OR LISTEN TO REPLY? A KEY ERROR IS A COACH FORMULATING THE NEXT QUESTION INSTEAD OF LISTENING.

8: IF YOU USED NO TOOLS OR TECHNIQUES TODAY HOW DID THAT MAKE YOU FEEL? DID YOU LEAVE THINKING YOU MISSED SOMETHING? WHAT COULD YOU CHANGE FOR NEXT TIME?

9: WHAT PERCENTAGE OF THE SESSION WAS DRIVEN BY YOU? HOW MUCH OF THE SESSION WERE YOU RELAXED AND NOTICED WHAT CAME UP IN THE SESSION?

10: HOW MUCH OF THE SESSION WAS ABOUT YOU AND HOW MUCH ABOUT THE CLIENT? HOW COULD YOU LOOK AT THIS IN MORE DETAIL?

DATE:-   /   /

1: HOW MUCH GUIDING VS TELLING DID YOU DO? WHO WAS THIS
FOR YOU OR THE CLIENT? WHAT COULD YOU DO DIFFERENTLY TO GROW?

2: WHAT MODELS HAVE YOU USED TODAY? BEHAVIOURAL MODELS OR
NOTICING EMOTIONS AND FEELINGS? WHAT COULD YOU THINK ABOUT
DIFFERENTLY FOR THE NEXT SESSION?

3: HOW MUCH OF YOUR WORK IS A HABIT? WHAT NEW HABITS WOULD
YOU LIKE TO CREATE AND WHAT ONES WOULD YOU LIKE TO DELETE LIKE
AN APP ON YOUR PHONE. THINK ABOUT ONE FOR YOUR NEXT SESSION.

4: HOW WAS YOUR CLIENT RELATIONSHIP TODAY, WHY WAS THIS?
WHAT WOULD YOU LIKE TO BE DIFFERENT?

5: WHAT TOOLS HAVE YOU USED TODAY, WHY? DID YOU PREPARE TO
USE THEM? IF THIS IS THE CASE WHAT MIGHT YOU HAVE MISSED BY NOT
PAYING ATTENTION? WHAT COULD YOU DO DIFFERENTLY NEXT TIME?

6: WHAT WAS YOUR STYLE TODAY? AUTOCRATIC (BOSSY AND AUTHORITIVE) DEMOCRATIC (GUIDE AND PERSONNEL), LAISSEZ-FAIRE (MINDFUL AND RELAXED). REFLECT ON THIS AND WATCH HOW YOU CHANGE, WHAT TRIGGERS YOUR STYLE?

7: HOW MUCH ACTIVE LISTENING DID YOU DO? DID YOU LISTEN TO UNDERSTAND OR LISTEN TO REPLY? A KEY ERROR IS A COACH FORMULATING THE NEXT QUESTION INSTEAD OF LISTENING.

8: IF YOU USED NO TOOLS OR TECHNIQUES TODAY HOW DID THAT MAKE YOU FEEL? DID YOU LEAVE THINKING YOU MISSED SOMETHING? WHAT COULD YOU CHANGE FOR NEXT TIME?

9: WHAT PERCENTAGE OF THE SESSION WAS DRIVEN BY YOU? HOW MUCH OF THE SESSION WERE YOU RELAXED AND NOTICED WHAT CAME UP IN THE SESSION?

10: HOW MUCH OF THE SESSION WAS ABOUT YOU AND HOW MUCH ABOUT THE CLIENT? HOW COULD YOU LOOK AT THIS IN MORE DETAIL?

DATE:-   /   /

1: HOW MUCH GUIDING VS TELLING DID YOU DO? WHO WAS THIS FOR YOU OR THE CLIENT? WHAT COULD YOU DO DIFFERENTLY TO GROW?

2: WHAT MODELS HAVE YOU USED TODAY? BEHAVIOURAL MODELS OR NOTICING EMOTIONS AND FEELINGS? WHAT COULD YOU THINK ABOUT DIFFERENTLY FOR THE NEXT SESSION?

3: HOW MUCH OF YOUR WORK IS A HABIT? WHAT NEW HABITS WOULD YOU LIKE TO CREATE AND WHAT ONES WOULD YOU LIKE TO DELETE LIKE AN APP ON YOUR PHONE. THINK ABOUT ONE FOR YOUR NEXT SESSION.

4: HOW WAS YOUR CLIENT RELATIONSHIP TODAY, WHY WAS THIS? WHAT WOULD YOU LIKE TO BE DIFFERENT?

5: WHAT TOOLS HAVE YOU USED TODAY, WHY? DID YOU PREPARE TO USE THEM? IF THIS IS THE CASE WHAT MIGHT YOU HAVE MISSED BY NOT PAYING ATTENTION? WHAT COULD YOU DO DIFFERENTLY NEXT TIME?

6: WHAT WAS YOUR STYLE TODAY? AUTOCRATIC (BOSSY AND AUTHORITIVE) DEMOCRATIC (GUIDE AND PERSONNEL), LAISSEZ-FAIRE (MINDFUL AND RELAXED). REFLECT ON THIS AND WATCH HOW YOU CHANGE, WHAT TRIGGERS YOUR STYLE?

7: HOW MUCH ACTIVE LISTENING DID YOU DO? DID YOU LISTEN TO UNDERSTAND OR LISTEN TO REPLY? A KEY ERROR IS A COACH FORMULATING THE NEXT QUESTION INSTEAD OF LISTENING.

8: IF YOU USED NO TOOLS OR TECHNIQUES TODAY HOW DID THAT MAKE YOU FEEL? DID YOU LEAVE THINKING YOU MISSED SOMETHING? WHAT COULD YOU CHANGE FOR NEXT TIME?

9: WHAT PERCENTAGE OF THE SESSION WAS DRIVEN BY YOU? HOW MUCH OF THE SESSION WERE YOU RELAXED AND NOTICED WHAT CAME UP IN THE SESSION?

10: HOW MUCH OF THE SESSION WAS ABOUT YOU AND HOW MUCH ABOUT THE CLIENT? HOW COULD YOU LOOK AT THIS IN MORE DETAIL?

DATE:-   /   /

1: HOW MUCH GUIDING VS TELLING DID YOU DO? WHO WAS THIS FOR YOU OR THE CLIENT? WHAT COULD YOU DO DIFFERENTLY TO GROW?

2: WHAT MODELS HAVE YOU USED TODAY? BEHAVIOURAL MODELS OR NOTICING EMOTIONS AND FEELINGS? WHAT COULD YOU THINK ABOUT DIFFERENTLY FOR THE NEXT SESSION?

3: HOW MUCH OF YOUR WORK IS A HABIT? WHAT NEW HABITS WOULD YOU LIKE TO CREATE AND WHAT ONES WOULD YOU LIKE TO DELETE LIKE AN APP ON YOUR PHONE. THINK ABOUT ONE FOR YOUR NEXT SESSION.

4: HOW WAS YOUR CLIENT RELATIONSHIP TODAY, WHY WAS THIS? WHAT WOULD YOU LIKE TO BE DIFFERENT?

5: WHAT TOOLS HAVE YOU USED TODAY, WHY? DID YOU PREPARE TO USE THEM? IF THIS IS THE CASE WHAT MIGHT YOU HAVE MISSED BY NOT PAYING ATTENTION? WHAT COULD YOU DO DIFFERENTLY NEXT TIME?

6: WHAT WAS YOUR STYLE TODAY? AUTOCRATIC (BOSSY AND AUTHORITIVE) DEMOCRATIC (GUIDE AND PERSONNEL), LAISSEZ-FAIRE (MINDFUL AND RELAXED). REFLECT ON THIS AND WATCH HOW YOU CHANGE, WHAT TRIGGERS YOUR STYLE?

7: HOW MUCH ACTIVE LISTENING DID YOU DO? DID YOU LISTEN TO UNDERSTAND OR LISTEN TO REPLY? A KEY ERROR IS A COACH FORMULATING THE NEXT QUESTION INSTEAD OF LISTENING.

8: IF YOU USED NO TOOLS OR TECHNIQUES TODAY HOW DID THAT MAKE YOU FEEL? DID YOU LEAVE THINKING YOU MISSED SOMETHING? WHAT COULD YOU CHANGE FOR NEXT TIME?

9: WHAT PERCENTAGE OF THE SESSION WAS DRIVEN BY YOU? HOW MUCH OF THE SESSION WERE YOU RELAXED AND NOTICED WHAT CAME UP IN THE SESSION?

10: HOW MUCH OF THE SESSION WAS ABOUT YOU AND HOW MUCH ABOUT THE CLIENT? HOW COULD YOU LOOK AT THIS IN MORE DETAIL?

DATE:-   /   /

1: HOW MUCH GUIDING VS TELLING DID YOU DO? WHO WAS THIS FOR YOU OR THE CLIENT? WHAT COULD YOU DO DIFFERENTLY TO GROW?

2: WHAT MODELS HAVE YOU USED TODAY? BEHAVIOURAL MODELS OR NOTICING EMOTIONS AND FEELINGS? WHAT COULD YOU THINK ABOUT DIFFERENTLY FOR THE NEXT SESSION?

3: HOW MUCH OF YOUR WORK IS A HABIT? WHAT NEW HABITS WOULD YOU LIKE TO CREATE AND WHAT ONES WOULD YOU LIKE TO DELETE LIKE AN APP ON YOUR PHONE. THINK ABOUT ONE FOR YOUR NEXT SESSION.

4: HOW WAS YOUR CLIENT RELATIONSHIP TODAY, WHY WAS THIS? WHAT WOULD YOU LIKE TO BE DIFFERENT?

5: WHAT TOOLS HAVE YOU USED TODAY, WHY? DID YOU PREPARE TO USE THEM? IF THIS IS THE CASE WHAT MIGHT YOU HAVE MISSED BY NOT PAYING ATTENTION? WHAT COULD YOU DO DIFFERENTLY NEXT TIME?

6: WHAT WAS YOUR STYLE TODAY? AUTOCRATIC (BOSSY AND AUTHORITIVE) DEMOCRATIC (GUIDE AND PERSONNEL), LAISSEZ-FAIRE (MINDFUL AND RELAXED). REFLECT ON THIS AND WATCH HOW YOU CHANGE, WHAT TRIGGERS YOUR STYLE?

7: HOW MUCH ACTIVE LISTENING DID YOU DO? DID YOU LISTEN TO UNDERSTAND OR LISTEN TO REPLY? A KEY ERROR IS A COACH FORMULATING THE NEXT QUESTION INSTEAD OF LISTENING.

8: IF YOU USED NO TOOLS OR TECHNIQUES TODAY HOW DID THAT MAKE YOU FEEL? DID YOU LEAVE THINKING YOU MISSED SOMETHING? WHAT COULD YOU CHANGE FOR NEXT TIME?

9: WHAT PERCENTAGE OF THE SESSION WAS DRIVEN BY YOU? HOW MUCH OF THE SESSION WERE YOU RELAXED AND NOTICED WHAT CAME UP IN THE SESSION?

10: HOW MUCH OF THE SESSION WAS ABOUT YOU AND HOW MUCH ABOUT THE CLIENT? HOW COULD YOU LOOK AT THIS IN MORE DETAIL?

DATE:-   /   /

1: HOW MUCH GUIDING VS TELLING DID YOU DO? WHO WAS THIS FOR YOU OR THE CLIENT? WHAT COULD YOU DO DIFFERENTLY TO GROW?

2: WHAT MODELS HAVE YOU USED TODAY? BEHAVIOURAL MODELS OR NOTICING EMOTIONS AND FEELINGS? WHAT COULD YOU THINK ABOUT DIFFERENTLY FOR THE NEXT SESSION?

3: HOW MUCH OF YOUR WORK IS A HABIT? WHAT NEW HABITS WOULD YOU LIKE TO CREATE AND WHAT ONES WOULD YOU LIKE TO DELETE LIKE AN APP ON YOUR PHONE. THINK ABOUT ONE FOR YOUR NEXT SESSION.

4: HOW WAS YOUR CLIENT RELATIONSHIP TODAY, WHY WAS THIS? WHAT WOULD YOU LIKE TO BE DIFFERENT?

5: WHAT TOOLS HAVE YOU USED TODAY, WHY? DID YOU PREPARE TO USE THEM? IF THIS IS THE CASE WHAT MIGHT YOU HAVE MISSED BY NOT PAYING ATTENTION? WHAT COULD YOU DO DIFFERENTLY NEXT TIME?

6: WHAT WAS YOUR STYLE TODAY? AUTOCRATIC (BOSSY AND AUTHORITIVE) DEMOCRATIC (GUIDE AND PERSONNEL), LAISSEZ-FAIRE (MINDFUL AND RELAXED). REFLECT ON THIS AND WATCH HOW YOU CHANGE, WHAT TRIGGERS YOUR STYLE?

7: HOW MUCH ACTIVE LISTENING DID YOU DO? DID YOU LISTEN TO UNDERSTAND OR LISTEN TO REPLY? A KEY ERROR IS A COACH FORMULATING THE NEXT QUESTION INSTEAD OF LISTENING.

8: IF YOU USED NO TOOLS OR TECHNIQUES TODAY HOW DID THAT MAKE YOU FEEL? DID YOU LEAVE THINKING YOU MISSED SOMETHING? WHAT COULD YOU CHANGE FOR NEXT TIME?

9: WHAT PERCENTAGE OF THE SESSION WAS DRIVEN BY YOU? HOW MUCH OF THE SESSION WERE YOU RELAXED AND NOTICED WHAT CAME UP IN THE SESSION?

10: HOW MUCH OF THE SESSION WAS ABOUT YOU AND HOW MUCH ABOUT THE CLIENT? HOW COULD YOU LOOK AT THIS IN MORE DETAIL?

DATE:-   /   /

1: HOW MUCH GUIDING VS TELLING DID YOU DO? WHO WAS THIS FOR YOU OR THE CLIENT? WHAT COULD YOU DO DIFFERENTLY TO GROW?

2: WHAT MODELS HAVE YOU USED TODAY? BEHAVIOURAL MODELS OR NOTICING EMOTIONS AND FEELINGS? WHAT COULD YOU THINK ABOUT DIFFERENTLY FOR THE NEXT SESSION?

3: HOW MUCH OF YOUR WORK IS A HABIT? WHAT NEW HABITS WOULD YOU LIKE TO CREATE AND WHAT ONES WOULD YOU LIKE TO DELETE LIKE AN APP ON YOUR PHONE. THINK ABOUT ONE FOR YOUR NEXT SESSION.

4: HOW WAS YOUR CLIENT RELATIONSHIP TODAY, WHY WAS THIS? WHAT WOULD YOU LIKE TO BE DIFFERENT?

5: WHAT TOOLS HAVE YOU USED TODAY, WHY? DID YOU PREPARE TO USE THEM? IF THIS IS THE CASE WHAT MIGHT YOU HAVE MISSED BY NOT PAYING ATTENTION? WHAT COULD YOU DO DIFFERENTLY NEXT TIME?

6: WHAT WAS YOUR STYLE TODAY? AUTOCRATIC (BOSSY AND AUTHORITIVE) DEMOCRATIC (GUIDE AND PERSONNEL), LAISSEZ-FAIRE (MINDFUL AND RELAXED). REFLECT ON THIS AND WATCH HOW YOU CHANGE, WHAT TRIGGERS YOUR STYLE?

7: HOW MUCH ACTIVE LISTENING DID YOU DO? DID YOU LISTEN TO UNDERSTAND OR LISTEN TO REPLY? A KEY ERROR IS A COACH FORMULATING THE NEXT QUESTION INSTEAD OF LISTENING.

8: IF YOU USED NO TOOLS OR TECHNIQUES TODAY HOW DID THAT MAKE YOU FEEL? DID YOU LEAVE THINKING YOU MISSED SOMETHING? WHAT COULD YOU CHANGE FOR NEXT TIME?

9: WHAT PERCENTAGE OF THE SESSION WAS DRIVEN BY YOU? HOW MUCH OF THE SESSION WERE YOU RELAXED AND NOTICED WHAT CAME UP IN THE SESSION?

10: HOW MUCH OF THE SESSION WAS ABOUT YOU AND HOW MUCH ABOUT THE CLIENT? HOW COULD YOU LOOK AT THIS IN MORE DETAIL?

DATE:-   /   /

1: HOW MUCH GUIDING VS TELLING DID YOU DO? WHO WAS THIS FOR YOU OR THE CLIENT? WHAT COULD YOU DO DIFFERENTLY TO GROW?

2: WHAT MODELS HAVE YOU USED TODAY? BEHAVIOURAL MODELS OR NOTICING EMOTIONS AND FEELINGS? WHAT COULD YOU THINK ABOUT DIFFERENTLY FOR THE NEXT SESSION?

3: HOW MUCH OF YOUR WORK IS A HABIT? WHAT NEW HABITS WOULD YOU LIKE TO CREATE AND WHAT ONES WOULD YOU LIKE TO DELETE LIKE AN APP ON YOUR PHONE. THINK ABOUT ONE FOR YOUR NEXT SESSION.

4: HOW WAS YOUR CLIENT RELATIONSHIP TODAY, WHY WAS THIS? WHAT WOULD YOU LIKE TO BE DIFFERENT?

5: WHAT TOOLS HAVE YOU USED TODAY, WHY? DID YOU PREPARE TO USE THEM? IF THIS IS THE CASE WHAT MIGHT YOU HAVE MISSED BY NOT PAYING ATTENTION? WHAT COULD YOU DO DIFFERENTLY NEXT TIME?

6: WHAT WAS YOUR STYLE TODAY? AUTOCRATIC (BOSSY AND AUTHORITIVE) DEMOCRATIC (GUIDE AND PERSONNEL), LAISSEZ-FAIRE (MINDFUL AND RELAXED). REFLECT ON THIS AND WATCH HOW YOU CHANGE, WHAT TRIGGERS YOUR STYLE?

7: HOW MUCH ACTIVE LISTENING DID YOU DO? DID YOU LISTEN TO UNDERSTAND OR LISTEN TO REPLY? A KEY ERROR IS A COACH FORMULATING THE NEXT QUESTION INSTEAD OF LISTENING.

8: IF YOU USED NO TOOLS OR TECHNIQUES TODAY HOW DID THAT MAKE YOU FEEL? DID YOU LEAVE THINKING YOU MISSED SOMETHING? WHAT COULD YOU CHANGE FOR NEXT TIME?

9: WHAT PERCENTAGE OF THE SESSION WAS DRIVEN BY YOU? HOW MUCH OF THE SESSION WERE YOU RELAXED AND NOTICED WHAT CAME UP IN THE SESSION?

10: HOW MUCH OF THE SESSION WAS ABOUT YOU AND HOW MUCH ABOUT THE CLIENT? HOW COULD YOU LOOK AT THIS IN MORE DETAIL?

DATE:-   /   /

1: HOW MUCH GUIDING VS TELLING DID YOU DO? WHO WAS THIS FOR YOU OR THE CLIENT? WHAT COULD YOU DO DIFFERENTLY TO GROW?

2: WHAT MODELS HAVE YOU USED TODAY? BEHAVIOURAL MODELS OR NOTICING EMOTIONS AND FEELINGS? WHAT COULD YOU THINK ABOUT DIFFERENTLY FOR THE NEXT SESSION?

3: HOW MUCH OF YOUR WORK IS A HABIT? WHAT NEW HABITS WOULD YOU LIKE TO CREATE AND WHAT ONES WOULD YOU LIKE TO DELETE LIKE AN APP ON YOUR PHONE. THINK ABOUT ONE FOR YOUR NEXT SESSION.

4: HOW WAS YOUR CLIENT RELATIONSHIP TODAY, WHY WAS THIS? WHAT WOULD YOU LIKE TO BE DIFFERENT?

5: WHAT TOOLS HAVE YOU USED TODAY, WHY? DID YOU PREPARE TO USE THEM? IF THIS IS THE CASE WHAT MIGHT YOU HAVE MISSED BY NOT PAYING ATTENTION? WHAT COULD YOU DO DIFFERENTLY NEXT TIME?

6: WHAT WAS YOUR STYLE TODAY? AUTOCRATIC (BOSSY AND AUTHORITIVE) DEMOCRATIC (GUIDE AND PERSONNEL), LAISSEZ-FAIRE (MINDFUL AND RELAXED). REFLECT ON THIS AND WATCH HOW YOU CHANGE, WHAT TRIGGERS YOUR STYLE?

7: HOW MUCH ACTIVE LISTENING DID YOU DO? DID YOU LISTEN TO UNDERSTAND OR LISTEN TO REPLY? A KEY ERROR IS A COACH FORMULATING THE NEXT QUESTION INSTEAD OF LISTENING.

8: IF YOU USED NO TOOLS OR TECHNIQUES TODAY HOW DID THAT MAKE YOU FEEL? DID YOU LEAVE THINKING YOU MISSED SOMETHING? WHAT COULD YOU CHANGE FOR NEXT TIME?

9: WHAT PERCENTAGE OF THE SESSION WAS DRIVEN BY YOU? HOW MUCH OF THE SESSION WERE YOU RELAXED AND NOTICED WHAT CAME UP IN THE SESSION?

10: HOW MUCH OF THE SESSION WAS ABOUT YOU AND HOW MUCH ABOUT THE CLIENT? HOW COULD YOU LOOK AT THIS IN MORE DETAIL?

DATE:-   /   /

1: HOW MUCH GUIDING VS TELLING DID YOU DO? WHO WAS THIS FOR YOU OR THE CLIENT? WHAT COULD YOU DO DIFFERENTLY TO GROW?

2: WHAT MODELS HAVE YOU USED TODAY? BEHAVIOURAL MODELS OR NOTICING EMOTIONS AND FEELINGS? WHAT COULD YOU THINK ABOUT DIFFERENTLY FOR THE NEXT SESSION?

3: HOW MUCH OF YOUR WORK IS A HABIT? WHAT NEW HABITS WOULD YOU LIKE TO CREATE AND WHAT ONES WOULD YOU LIKE TO DELETE LIKE AN APP ON YOUR PHONE. THINK ABOUT ONE FOR YOUR NEXT SESSION.

4: HOW WAS YOUR CLIENT RELATIONSHIP TODAY, WHY WAS THIS? WHAT WOULD YOU LIKE TO BE DIFFERENT?

5: WHAT TOOLS HAVE YOU USED TODAY, WHY? DID YOU PREPARE TO USE THEM? IF THIS IS THE CASE WHAT MIGHT YOU HAVE MISSED BY NOT PAYING ATTENTION? WHAT COULD YOU DO DIFFERENTLY NEXT TIME?

6: WHAT WAS YOUR STYLE TODAY? AUTOCRATIC (BOSSY AND AUTHORITIVE) DEMOCRATIC (GUIDE AND PERSONNEL), LAISSEZ-FAIRE (MINDFUL AND RELAXED). REFLECT ON THIS AND WATCH HOW YOU CHANGE, WHAT TRIGGERS YOUR STYLE?

7: HOW MUCH ACTIVE LISTENING DID YOU DO? DID YOU LISTEN TO UNDERSTAND OR LISTEN TO REPLY? A KEY ERROR IS A COACH FORMULATING THE NEXT QUESTION INSTEAD OF LISTENING.

8: IF YOU USED NO TOOLS OR TECHNIQUES TODAY HOW DID THAT MAKE YOU FEEL? DID YOU LEAVE THINKING YOU MISSED SOMETHING? WHAT COULD YOU CHANGE FOR NEXT TIME?

9: WHAT PERCENTAGE OF THE SESSION WAS DRIVEN BY YOU? HOW MUCH OF THE SESSION WERE YOU RELAXED AND NOTICED WHAT CAME UP IN THE SESSION?

10: HOW MUCH OF THE SESSION WAS ABOUT YOU AND HOW MUCH ABOUT THE CLIENT? HOW COULD YOU LOOK AT THIS IN MORE DETAIL?

1: HOW HAVE I GROWN OVER THE LAST 10 DAYS

2: WHAT AM I GOING TO FOCUS ON OVER THE NEXT 10 DAYS?

**3: WHAT FIVE THINGS AM I POSITIVELY TAKING FROM THE LAST 10
DAYS AND MOVING THEM FORWARD INTO THE NEXT 10 DAYS.**

-
-
-
-
-

4: WHAT KEY AREAS WOULD I LIKE TO CONCENTRATE ON?

"Discover your gift, develop your gift, and then give it away every day."

DON MEYER

DATE:-   /   /

1: HOW MUCH GUIDING VS TELLING DID YOU DO? WHO WAS THIS FOR YOU OR THE CLIENT? WHAT COULD YOU DO DIFFERENTLY TO GROW?

2: WHAT MODELS HAVE YOU USED TODAY? BEHAVIOURAL MODELS OR NOTICING EMOTIONS AND FEELINGS? WHAT COULD YOU THINK ABOUT DIFFERENTLY FOR THE NEXT SESSION?

3: HOW MUCH OF YOUR WORK IS A HABIT? WHAT NEW HABITS WOULD YOU LIKE TO CREATE AND WHAT ONES WOULD YOU LIKE TO DELETE LIKE AN APP ON YOUR PHONE. THINK ABOUT ONE FOR YOUR NEXT SESSION.

4: HOW WAS YOUR CLIENT RELATIONSHIP TODAY, WHY WAS THIS? WHAT WOULD YOU LIKE TO BE DIFFERENT?

5: WHAT TOOLS HAVE YOU USED TODAY, WHY? DID YOU PREPARE TO USE THEM? IF THIS IS THE CASE WHAT MIGHT YOU HAVE MISSED BY NOT PAYING ATTENTION? WHAT COULD YOU DO DIFFERENTLY NEXT TIME?

REFLECTION ON YOUR USE OF TOOLS AND TECHNIQUES IN COACHING

6: WHAT WAS YOUR STYLE TODAY? AUTOCRATIC (BOSSY AND AUTHORITIVE) DEMOCRATIC (GUIDE AND PERSONNEL), LAISSEZ-FAIRE (MINDFUL AND RELAXED). REFLECT ON THIS AND WATCH HOW YOU CHANGE, WHAT TRIGGERS YOUR STYLE?

7: HOW MUCH ACTIVE LISTENING DID YOU DO? DID YOU LISTEN TO UNDERSTAND OR LISTEN TO REPLY? A KEY ERROR IS A COACH FORMULATING THE NEXT QUESTION INSTEAD OF LISTENING.

8: IF YOU USED NO TOOLS OR TECHNIQUES TODAY HOW DID THAT MAKE YOU FEEL? DID YOU LEAVE THINKING YOU MISSED SOMETHING? WHAT COULD YOU CHANGE FOR NEXT TIME?

9: WHAT PERCENTAGE OF THE SESSION WAS DRIVEN BY YOU? HOW MUCH OF THE SESSION WERE YOU RELAXED AND NOTICED WHAT CAME UP IN THE SESSION?

10: HOW MUCH OF THE SESSION WAS ABOUT YOU AND HOW MUCH ABOUT THE CLIENT? HOW COULD YOU LOOK AT THIS IN MORE DETAIL?

DATE:-   /   /

1: HOW MUCH GUIDING VS TELLING DID YOU DO? WHO WAS THIS FOR YOU OR THE CLIENT? WHAT COULD YOU DO DIFFERENTLY TO GROW?

2: WHAT MODELS HAVE YOU USED TODAY? BEHAVIOURAL MODELS OR NOTICING EMOTIONS AND FEELINGS? WHAT COULD YOU THINK ABOUT DIFFERENTLY FOR THE NEXT SESSION?

3: HOW MUCH OF YOUR WORK IS A HABIT? WHAT NEW HABITS WOULD YOU LIKE TO CREATE AND WHAT ONES WOULD YOU LIKE TO DELETE LIKE AN APP ON YOUR PHONE. THINK ABOUT ONE FOR YOUR NEXT SESSION.

4: HOW WAS YOUR CLIENT RELATIONSHIP TODAY, WHY WAS THIS? WHAT WOULD YOU LIKE TO BE DIFFERENT?

5: WHAT TOOLS HAVE YOU USED TODAY, WHY? DID YOU PREPARE TO USE THEM? IF THIS IS THE CASE WHAT MIGHT YOU HAVE MISSED BY NOT PAYING ATTENTION? WHAT COULD YOU DO DIFFERENTLY NEXT TIME?

6: WHAT WAS YOUR STYLE TODAY? AUTOCRATIC (BOSSY AND AUTHORITIVE) DEMOCRATIC (GUIDE AND PERSONNEL), LAISSEZ-FAIRE (MINDFUL AND RELAXED). REFLECT ON THIS AND WATCH HOW YOU CHANGE, WHAT TRIGGERS YOUR STYLE?

7: HOW MUCH ACTIVE LISTENING DID YOU DO? DID YOU LISTEN TO UNDERSTAND OR LISTEN TO REPLY? A KEY ERROR IS A COACH FORMULATING THE NEXT QUESTION INSTEAD OF LISTENING.

8: IF YOU USED NO TOOLS OR TECHNIQUES TODAY HOW DID THAT MAKE YOU FEEL? DID YOU LEAVE THINKING YOU MISSED SOMETHING? WHAT COULD YOU CHANGE FOR NEXT TIME?

9: WHAT PERCENTAGE OF THE SESSION WAS DRIVEN BY YOU? HOW MUCH OF THE SESSION WERE YOU RELAXED AND NOTICED WHAT CAME UP IN THE SESSION?

10: HOW MUCH OF THE SESSION WAS ABOUT YOU AND HOW MUCH ABOUT THE CLIENT? HOW COULD YOU LOOK AT THIS IN MORE DETAIL?

DATE:-   /   /

1: HOW MUCH GUIDING VS TELLING DID YOU DO? WHO WAS THIS
FOR YOU OR THE CLIENT? WHAT COULD YOU DO DIFFERENTLY TO GROW?

2: WHAT MODELS HAVE YOU USED TODAY? BEHAVIOURAL MODELS OR
NOTICING EMOTIONS AND FEELINGS? WHAT COULD YOU THINK ABOUT
DIFFERENTLY FOR THE NEXT SESSION?

3: HOW MUCH OF YOUR WORK IS A HABIT? WHAT NEW HABITS WOULD
YOU LIKE TO CREATE AND WHAT ONES WOULD YOU LIKE TO DELETE LIKE
AN APP ON YOUR PHONE. THINK ABOUT ONE FOR YOUR NEXT SESSION.

4: HOW WAS YOUR CLIENT RELATIONSHIP TODAY, WHY WAS THIS?
WHAT WOULD YOU LIKE TO BE DIFFERENT?

5: WHAT TOOLS HAVE YOU USED TODAY, WHY? DID YOU PREPARE TO
USE THEM? IF THIS IS THE CASE WHAT MIGHT YOU HAVE MISSED BY NOT
PAYING ATTENTION? WHAT COULD YOU DO DIFFERENTLY NEXT TIME?

6: WHAT WAS YOUR STYLE TODAY? AUTOCRATIC (BOSSY AND AUTHORITIVE) DEMOCRATIC (GUIDE AND PERSONNEL), LAISSEZ-FAIRE (MINDFUL AND RELAXED). REFLECT ON THIS AND WATCH HOW YOU CHANGE, WHAT TRIGGERS YOUR STYLE?

7: HOW MUCH ACTIVE LISTENING DID YOU DO? DID YOU LISTEN TO UNDERSTAND OR LISTEN TO REPLY? A KEY ERROR IS A COACH FORMULATING THE NEXT QUESTION INSTEAD OF LISTENING.

8: IF YOU USED NO TOOLS OR TECHNIQUES TODAY HOW DID THAT MAKE YOU FEEL? DID YOU LEAVE THINKING YOU MISSED SOMETHING? WHAT COULD YOU CHANGE FOR NEXT TIME?

9: WHAT PERCENTAGE OF THE SESSION WAS DRIVEN BY YOU? HOW MUCH OF THE SESSION WERE YOU RELAXED AND NOTICED WHAT CAME UP IN THE SESSION?

10: HOW MUCH OF THE SESSION WAS ABOUT YOU AND HOW MUCH ABOUT THE CLIENT? HOW COULD YOU LOOK AT THIS IN MORE DETAIL?

DATE:-   /   /

1: HOW MUCH GUIDING VS TELLING DID YOU DO? WHO WAS THIS
FOR YOU OR THE CLIENT? WHAT COULD YOU DO DIFFERENTLY TO GROW?

2: WHAT MODELS HAVE YOU USED TODAY? BEHAVIOURAL MODELS OR
NOTICING EMOTIONS AND FEELINGS? WHAT COULD YOU THINK ABOUT
DIFFERENTLY FOR THE NEXT SESSION?

3: HOW MUCH OF YOUR WORK IS A HABIT? WHAT NEW HABITS WOULD
YOU LIKE TO CREATE AND WHAT ONES WOULD YOU LIKE TO DELETE LIKE
AN APP ON YOUR PHONE. THINK ABOUT ONE FOR YOUR NEXT SESSION.

4: HOW WAS YOUR CLIENT RELATIONSHIP TODAY, WHY WAS THIS?
WHAT WOULD YOU LIKE TO BE DIFFERENT?

5: WHAT TOOLS HAVE YOU USED TODAY, WHY? DID YOU PREPARE TO
USE THEM? IF THIS IS THE CASE WHAT MIGHT YOU HAVE MISSED BY NOT
PAYING ATTENTION? WHAT COULD YOU DO DIFFERENTLY NEXT TIME?

6: WHAT WAS YOUR STYLE TODAY? AUTOCRATIC (BOSSY AND AUTHORITIVE) DEMOCRATIC (GUIDE AND PERSONNEL), LAISSEZ-FAIRE (MINDFUL AND RELAXED). REFLECT ON THIS AND WATCH HOW YOU CHANGE, WHAT TRIGGERS YOUR STYLE?

7: HOW MUCH ACTIVE LISTENING DID YOU DO? DID YOU LISTEN TO UNDERSTAND OR LISTEN TO REPLY? A KEY ERROR IS A COACH FORMULATING THE NEXT QUESTION INSTEAD OF LISTENING.

8: IF YOU USED NO TOOLS OR TECHNIQUES TODAY HOW DID THAT MAKE YOU FEEL? DID YOU LEAVE THINKING YOU MISSED SOMETHING? WHAT COULD YOU CHANGE FOR NEXT TIME?

9: WHAT PERCENTAGE OF THE SESSION WAS DRIVEN BY YOU? HOW MUCH OF THE SESSION WERE YOU RELAXED AND NOTICED WHAT CAME UP IN THE SESSION?

10: HOW MUCH OF THE SESSION WAS ABOUT YOU AND HOW MUCH ABOUT THE CLIENT? HOW COULD YOU LOOK AT THIS IN MORE DETAIL?

DATE:-   /   /

1: HOW MUCH GUIDING VS TELLING DID YOU DO? WHO WAS THIS FOR YOU OR THE CLIENT? WHAT COULD YOU DO DIFFERENTLY TO GROW?

2: WHAT MODELS HAVE YOU USED TODAY? BEHAVIOURAL MODELS OR NOTICING EMOTIONS AND FEELINGS? WHAT COULD YOU THINK ABOUT DIFFERENTLY FOR THE NEXT SESSION?

3: HOW MUCH OF YOUR WORK IS A HABIT? WHAT NEW HABITS WOULD YOU LIKE TO CREATE AND WHAT ONES WOULD YOU LIKE TO DELETE LIKE AN APP ON YOUR PHONE. THINK ABOUT ONE FOR YOUR NEXT SESSION.

4: HOW WAS YOUR CLIENT RELATIONSHIP TODAY, WHY WAS THIS? WHAT WOULD YOU LIKE TO BE DIFFERENT?

5: WHAT TOOLS HAVE YOU USED TODAY, WHY? DID YOU PREPARE TO USE THEM? IF THIS IS THE CASE WHAT MIGHT YOU HAVE MISSED BY NOT PAYING ATTENTION? WHAT COULD YOU DO DIFFERENTLY NEXT TIME?

6: WHAT WAS YOUR STYLE TODAY? AUTOCRATIC (BOSSY AND AUTHORITIVE) DEMOCRATIC (GUIDE AND PERSONNEL), LAISSEZ-FAIRE (MINDFUL AND RELAXED). REFLECT ON THIS AND WATCH HOW YOU CHANGE, WHAT TRIGGERS YOUR STYLE?

7: HOW MUCH ACTIVE LISTENING DID YOU DO? DID YOU LISTEN TO UNDERSTAND OR LISTEN TO REPLY? A KEY ERROR IS A COACH FORMULATING THE NEXT QUESTION INSTEAD OF LISTENING.

8: IF YOU USED NO TOOLS OR TECHNIQUES TODAY HOW DID THAT MAKE YOU FEEL? DID YOU LEAVE THINKING YOU MISSED SOMETHING? WHAT COULD YOU CHANGE FOR NEXT TIME?

9: WHAT PERCENTAGE OF THE SESSION WAS DRIVEN BY YOU? HOW MUCH OF THE SESSION WERE YOU RELAXED AND NOTICED WHAT CAME UP IN THE SESSION?

10: HOW MUCH OF THE SESSION WAS ABOUT YOU AND HOW MUCH ABOUT THE CLIENT? HOW COULD YOU LOOK AT THIS IN MORE DETAIL?

DATE:-   /   /

1: HOW MUCH GUIDING VS TELLING DID YOU DO? WHO WAS THIS FOR YOU OR THE CLIENT? WHAT COULD YOU DO DIFFERENTLY TO GROW?

2: WHAT MODELS HAVE YOU USED TODAY? BEHAVIOURAL MODELS OR NOTICING EMOTIONS AND FEELINGS? WHAT COULD YOU THINK ABOUT DIFFERENTLY FOR THE NEXT SESSION?

3: HOW MUCH OF YOUR WORK IS A HABIT? WHAT NEW HABITS WOULD YOU LIKE TO CREATE AND WHAT ONES WOULD YOU LIKE TO DELETE LIKE AN APP ON YOUR PHONE. THINK ABOUT ONE FOR YOUR NEXT SESSION.

4: HOW WAS YOUR CLIENT RELATIONSHIP TODAY, WHY WAS THIS? WHAT WOULD YOU LIKE TO BE DIFFERENT?

5: WHAT TOOLS HAVE YOU USED TODAY, WHY? DID YOU PREPARE TO USE THEM? IF THIS IS THE CASE WHAT MIGHT YOU HAVE MISSED BY NOT PAYING ATTENTION? WHAT COULD YOU DO DIFFERENTLY NEXT TIME?

6: WHAT WAS YOUR STYLE TODAY? AUTOCRATIC (BOSSY AND AUTHORITIVE) DEMOCRATIC (GUIDE AND PERSONNEL), LAISSEZ-FAIRE (MINDFUL AND RELAXED). REFLECT ON THIS AND WATCH HOW YOU CHANGE, WHAT TRIGGERS YOUR STYLE?

7: HOW MUCH ACTIVE LISTENING DID YOU DO? DID YOU LISTEN TO UNDERSTAND OR LISTEN TO REPLY? A KEY ERROR IS A COACH FORMULATING THE NEXT QUESTION INSTEAD OF LISTENING.

8: IF YOU USED NO TOOLS OR TECHNIQUES TODAY HOW DID THAT MAKE YOU FEEL? DID YOU LEAVE THINKING YOU MISSED SOMETHING? WHAT COULD YOU CHANGE FOR NEXT TIME?

9: WHAT PERCENTAGE OF THE SESSION WAS DRIVEN BY YOU? HOW MUCH OF THE SESSION WERE YOU RELAXED AND NOTICED WHAT CAME UP IN THE SESSION?

10: HOW MUCH OF THE SESSION WAS ABOUT YOU AND HOW MUCH ABOUT THE CLIENT? HOW COULD YOU LOOK AT THIS IN MORE DETAIL?

DATE:-   /   /

1: HOW MUCH GUIDING VS TELLING DID YOU DO? WHO WAS THIS FOR YOU OR THE CLIENT? WHAT COULD YOU DO DIFFERENTLY TO GROW?

2: WHAT MODELS HAVE YOU USED TODAY? BEHAVIOURAL MODELS OR NOTICING EMOTIONS AND FEELINGS? WHAT COULD YOU THINK ABOUT DIFFERENTLY FOR THE NEXT SESSION?

3: HOW MUCH OF YOUR WORK IS A HABIT? WHAT NEW HABITS WOULD YOU LIKE TO CREATE AND WHAT ONES WOULD YOU LIKE TO DELETE LIKE AN APP ON YOUR PHONE. THINK ABOUT ONE FOR YOUR NEXT SESSION.

4: HOW WAS YOUR CLIENT RELATIONSHIP TODAY, WHY WAS THIS? WHAT WOULD YOU LIKE TO BE DIFFERENT?

5: WHAT TOOLS HAVE YOU USED TODAY, WHY? DID YOU PREPARE TO USE THEM? IF THIS IS THE CASE WHAT MIGHT YOU HAVE MISSED BY NOT PAYING ATTENTION? WHAT COULD YOU DO DIFFERENTLY NEXT TIME?

6: WHAT WAS YOUR STYLE TODAY? AUTOCRATIC (BOSSY AND AUTHORITIVE) DEMOCRATIC (GUIDE AND PERSONNEL), LAISSEZ-FAIRE (MINDFUL AND RELAXED). REFLECT ON THIS AND WATCH HOW YOU CHANGE, WHAT TRIGGERS YOUR STYLE?

7: HOW MUCH ACTIVE LISTENING DID YOU DO? DID YOU LISTEN TO UNDERSTAND OR LISTEN TO REPLY? A KEY ERROR IS A COACH FORMULATING THE NEXT QUESTION INSTEAD OF LISTENING.

8: IF YOU USED NO TOOLS OR TECHNIQUES TODAY HOW DID THAT MAKE YOU FEEL? DID YOU LEAVE THINKING YOU MISSED SOMETHING? WHAT COULD YOU CHANGE FOR NEXT TIME?

9: WHAT PERCENTAGE OF THE SESSION WAS DRIVEN BY YOU? HOW MUCH OF THE SESSION WERE YOU RELAXED AND NOTICED WHAT CAME UP IN THE SESSION?

10: HOW MUCH OF THE SESSION WAS ABOUT YOU AND HOW MUCH ABOUT THE CLIENT? HOW COULD YOU LOOK AT THIS IN MORE DETAIL?

DATE:-   /   /

1: HOW MUCH GUIDING VS TELLING DID YOU DO? WHO WAS THIS
FOR YOU OR THE CLIENT? WHAT COULD YOU DO DIFFERENTLY TO GROW?

2: WHAT MODELS HAVE YOU USED TODAY? BEHAVIOURAL MODELS OR
NOTICING EMOTIONS AND FEELINGS? WHAT COULD YOU THINK ABOUT
DIFFERENTLY FOR THE NEXT SESSION?

3: HOW MUCH OF YOUR WORK IS A HABIT? WHAT NEW HABITS WOULD
YOU LIKE TO CREATE AND WHAT ONES WOULD YOU LIKE TO DELETE LIKE
AN APP ON YOUR PHONE. THINK ABOUT ONE FOR YOUR NEXT SESSION.

4: HOW WAS YOUR CLIENT RELATIONSHIP TODAY, WHY WAS THIS?
WHAT WOULD YOU LIKE TO BE DIFFERENT?

5: WHAT TOOLS HAVE YOU USED TODAY, WHY? DID YOU PREPARE TO
USE THEM? IF THIS IS THE CASE WHAT MIGHT YOU HAVE MISSED BY NOT
PAYING ATTENTION? WHAT COULD YOU DO DIFFERENTLY NEXT TIME?

6: WHAT WAS YOUR STYLE TODAY? AUTOCRATIC (BOSSY AND AUTHORITIVE) DEMOCRATIC (GUIDE AND PERSONNEL), LAISSEZ-FAIRE (MINDFUL AND RELAXED). REFLECT ON THIS AND WATCH HOW YOU CHANGE, WHAT TRIGGERS YOUR STYLE?

7: HOW MUCH ACTIVE LISTENING DID YOU DO? DID YOU LISTEN TO UNDERSTAND OR LISTEN TO REPLY? A KEY ERROR IS A COACH FORMULATING THE NEXT QUESTION INSTEAD OF LISTENING.

8: IF YOU USED NO TOOLS OR TECHNIQUES TODAY HOW DID THAT MAKE YOU FEEL? DID YOU LEAVE THINKING YOU MISSED SOMETHING? WHAT COULD YOU CHANGE FOR NEXT TIME?

9: WHAT PERCENTAGE OF THE SESSION WAS DRIVEN BY YOU? HOW MUCH OF THE SESSION WERE YOU RELAXED AND NOTICED WHAT CAME UP IN THE SESSION?

10: HOW MUCH OF THE SESSION WAS ABOUT YOU AND HOW MUCH ABOUT THE CLIENT? HOW COULD YOU LOOK AT THIS IN MORE DETAIL?

DATE:-   /   /

1: HOW MUCH GUIDING VS TELLING DID YOU DO? WHO WAS THIS FOR YOU OR THE CLIENT? WHAT COULD YOU DO DIFFERENTLY TO GROW?

2: WHAT MODELS HAVE YOU USED TODAY? BEHAVIOURAL MODELS OR NOTICING EMOTIONS AND FEELINGS? WHAT COULD YOU THINK ABOUT DIFFERENTLY FOR THE NEXT SESSION?

3: HOW MUCH OF YOUR WORK IS A HABIT? WHAT NEW HABITS WOULD YOU LIKE TO CREATE AND WHAT ONES WOULD YOU LIKE TO DELETE LIKE AN APP ON YOUR PHONE. THINK ABOUT ONE FOR YOUR NEXT SESSION.

4: HOW WAS YOUR CLIENT RELATIONSHIP TODAY, WHY WAS THIS? WHAT WOULD YOU LIKE TO BE DIFFERENT?

5: WHAT TOOLS HAVE YOU USED TODAY, WHY? DID YOU PREPARE TO USE THEM? IF THIS IS THE CASE WHAT MIGHT YOU HAVE MISSED BY NOT PAYING ATTENTION? WHAT COULD YOU DO DIFFERENTLY NEXT TIME?

6: WHAT WAS YOUR STYLE TODAY? AUTOCRATIC (BOSSY AND AUTHORITIVE) DEMOCRATIC (GUIDE AND PERSONNEL), LAISSEZ-FAIRE (MINDFUL AND RELAXED). REFLECT ON THIS AND WATCH HOW YOU CHANGE, WHAT TRIGGERS YOUR STYLE?

7: HOW MUCH ACTIVE LISTENING DID YOU DO? DID YOU LISTEN TO UNDERSTAND OR LISTEN TO REPLY? A KEY ERROR IS A COACH FORMULATING THE NEXT QUESTION INSTEAD OF LISTENING.

8: IF YOU USED NO TOOLS OR TECHNIQUES TODAY HOW DID THAT MAKE YOU FEEL? DID YOU LEAVE THINKING YOU MISSED SOMETHING? WHAT COULD YOU CHANGE FOR NEXT TIME?

9: WHAT PERCENTAGE OF THE SESSION WAS DRIVEN BY YOU? HOW MUCH OF THE SESSION WERE YOU RELAXED AND NOTICED WHAT CAME UP IN THE SESSION?

10: HOW MUCH OF THE SESSION WAS ABOUT YOU AND HOW MUCH ABOUT THE CLIENT? HOW COULD YOU LOOK AT THIS IN MORE DETAIL?

DATE:-   /   /

1: HOW MUCH GUIDING VS TELLING DID YOU DO? WHO WAS THIS FOR YOU OR THE CLIENT? WHAT COULD YOU DO DIFFERENTLY TO GROW?

2: WHAT MODELS HAVE YOU USED TODAY? BEHAVIOURAL MODELS OR NOTICING EMOTIONS AND FEELINGS? WHAT COULD YOU THINK ABOUT DIFFERENTLY FOR THE NEXT SESSION?

3: HOW MUCH OF YOUR WORK IS A HABIT? WHAT NEW HABITS WOULD YOU LIKE TO CREATE AND WHAT ONES WOULD YOU LIKE TO DELETE LIKE AN APP ON YOUR PHONE. THINK ABOUT ONE FOR YOUR NEXT SESSION.

4: HOW WAS YOUR CLIENT RELATIONSHIP TODAY, WHY WAS THIS? WHAT WOULD YOU LIKE TO BE DIFFERENT?

5: WHAT TOOLS HAVE YOU USED TODAY, WHY? DID YOU PREPARE TO USE THEM? IF THIS IS THE CASE WHAT MIGHT YOU HAVE MISSED BY NOT PAYING ATTENTION? WHAT COULD YOU DO DIFFERENTLY NEXT TIME?

6: WHAT WAS YOUR STYLE TODAY? AUTOCRATIC (BOSSY AND AUTHORITIVE) DEMOCRATIC (GUIDE AND PERSONNEL), LAISSEZ-FAIRE (MINDFUL AND RELAXED). REFLECT ON THIS AND WATCH HOW YOU CHANGE, WHAT TRIGGERS YOUR STYLE?

7: HOW MUCH ACTIVE LISTENING DID YOU DO? DID YOU LISTEN TO UNDERSTAND OR LISTEN TO REPLY? A KEY ERROR IS A COACH FORMULATING THE NEXT QUESTION INSTEAD OF LISTENING.

8: IF YOU USED NO TOOLS OR TECHNIQUES TODAY HOW DID THAT MAKE YOU FEEL? DID YOU LEAVE THINKING YOU MISSED SOMETHING? WHAT COULD YOU CHANGE FOR NEXT TIME?

9: WHAT PERCENTAGE OF THE SESSION WAS DRIVEN BY YOU? HOW MUCH OF THE SESSION WERE YOU RELAXED AND NOTICED WHAT CAME UP IN THE SESSION?

10: HOW MUCH OF THE SESSION WAS ABOUT YOU AND HOW MUCH ABOUT THE CLIENT? HOW COULD YOU LOOK AT THIS IN MORE DETAIL?

1: HOW HAVE I GROWN OVER THE LAST 10 DAYS

2: WHAT AM I GOING TO FOCUS ON OVER THE NEXT 10 DAYS?

3: WHAT FIVE THINGS AM I POSITIVELY TAKING FROM THE LAST 10 DAYS AND MOVING THEM FORWARD INTO THE NEXT 10 DAYS.

-
-
-
-
-

4: WHAT KEY AREAS WOULD I LIKE TO CONCENTRATE ON?

"**Success is peace of mind which is a direct result of self-satisfaction in knowing you did your best to become the best you are capable of becoming.**"

JOHN WOODEN

DATE:-   /   /

1: HOW MUCH GUIDING VS TELLING DID YOU DO? WHO WAS THIS FOR YOU OR THE CLIENT? WHAT COULD YOU DO DIFFERENTLY TO GROW?

2: WHAT MODELS HAVE YOU USED TODAY? BEHAVIOURAL MODELS OR NOTICING EMOTIONS AND FEELINGS? WHAT COULD YOU THINK ABOUT DIFFERENTLY FOR THE NEXT SESSION?

3: HOW MUCH OF YOUR WORK IS A HABIT? WHAT NEW HABITS WOULD YOU LIKE TO CREATE AND WHAT ONES WOULD YOU LIKE TO DELETE LIKE AN APP ON YOUR PHONE. THINK ABOUT ONE FOR YOUR NEXT SESSION.

4: HOW WAS YOUR CLIENT RELATIONSHIP TODAY, WHY WAS THIS? WHAT WOULD YOU LIKE TO BE DIFFERENT?

5: WHAT TOOLS HAVE YOU USED TODAY, WHY? DID YOU PREPARE TO USE THEM? IF THIS IS THE CASE WHAT MIGHT YOU HAVE MISSED BY NOT PAYING ATTENTION? WHAT COULD YOU DO DIFFERENTLY NEXT TIME?

6: WHAT WAS YOUR STYLE TODAY? AUTOCRATIC (BOSSY AND AUTHORITIVE) DEMOCRATIC (GUIDE AND PERSONNEL), LAISSEZ-FAIRE (MINDFUL AND RELAXED). REFLECT ON THIS AND WATCH HOW YOU CHANGE, WHAT TRIGGERS YOUR STYLE?

7: HOW MUCH ACTIVE LISTENING DID YOU DO? DID YOU LISTEN TO UNDERSTAND OR LISTEN TO REPLY? A KEY ERROR IS A COACH FORMULATING THE NEXT QUESTION INSTEAD OF LISTENING.

8: IF YOU USED NO TOOLS OR TECHNIQUES TODAY HOW DID THAT MAKE YOU FEEL? DID YOU LEAVE THINKING YOU MISSED SOMETHING? WHAT COULD YOU CHANGE FOR NEXT TIME?

9: WHAT PERCENTAGE OF THE SESSION WAS DRIVEN BY YOU? HOW MUCH OF THE SESSION WERE YOU RELAXED AND NOTICED WHAT CAME UP IN THE SESSION?

10: HOW MUCH OF THE SESSION WAS ABOUT YOU AND HOW MUCH ABOUT THE CLIENT? HOW COULD YOU LOOK AT THIS IN MORE DETAIL?

DATE:- / /

1: HOW MUCH GUIDING VS TELLING DID YOU DO? WHO WAS THIS FOR YOU OR THE CLIENT? WHAT COULD YOU DO DIFFERENTLY TO GROW?

2: WHAT MODELS HAVE YOU USED TODAY? BEHAVIOURAL MODELS OR NOTICING EMOTIONS AND FEELINGS? WHAT COULD YOU THINK ABOUT DIFFERENTLY FOR THE NEXT SESSION?

3: HOW MUCH OF YOUR WORK IS A HABIT? WHAT NEW HABITS WOULD YOU LIKE TO CREATE AND WHAT ONES WOULD YOU LIKE TO DELETE LIKE AN APP ON YOUR PHONE. THINK ABOUT ONE FOR YOUR NEXT SESSION.

4: HOW WAS YOUR CLIENT RELATIONSHIP TODAY, WHY WAS THIS? WHAT WOULD YOU LIKE TO BE DIFFERENT?

5: WHAT TOOLS HAVE YOU USED TODAY, WHY? DID YOU PREPARE TO USE THEM? IF THIS IS THE CASE WHAT MIGHT YOU HAVE MISSED BY NOT PAYING ATTENTION? WHAT COULD YOU DO DIFFERENTLY NEXT TIME?

6: WHAT WAS YOUR STYLE TODAY? AUTOCRATIC (BOSSY AND AUTHORITIVE) DEMOCRATIC (GUIDE AND PERSONNEL), LAISSEZ-FAIRE (MINDFUL AND RELAXED). REFLECT ON THIS AND WATCH HOW YOU CHANGE, WHAT TRIGGERS YOUR STYLE?

7: HOW MUCH ACTIVE LISTENING DID YOU DO? DID YOU LISTEN TO UNDERSTAND OR LISTEN TO REPLY? A KEY ERROR IS A COACH FORMULATING THE NEXT QUESTION INSTEAD OF LISTENING.

8: IF YOU USED NO TOOLS OR TECHNIQUES TODAY HOW DID THAT MAKE YOU FEEL? DID YOU LEAVE THINKING YOU MISSED SOMETHING? WHAT COULD YOU CHANGE FOR NEXT TIME?

9: WHAT PERCENTAGE OF THE SESSION WAS DRIVEN BY YOU? HOW MUCH OF THE SESSION WERE YOU RELAXED AND NOTICED WHAT CAME UP IN THE SESSION?

10: HOW MUCH OF THE SESSION WAS ABOUT YOU AND HOW MUCH ABOUT THE CLIENT? HOW COULD YOU LOOK AT THIS IN MORE DETAIL?

DATE:-   /   /

1: HOW MUCH GUIDING VS TELLING DID YOU DO? WHO WAS THIS FOR YOU OR THE CLIENT? WHAT COULD YOU DO DIFFERENTLY TO GROW?

2: WHAT MODELS HAVE YOU USED TODAY? BEHAVIOURAL MODELS OR NOTICING EMOTIONS AND FEELINGS? WHAT COULD YOU THINK ABOUT DIFFERENTLY FOR THE NEXT SESSION?

3: HOW MUCH OF YOUR WORK IS A HABIT? WHAT NEW HABITS WOULD YOU LIKE TO CREATE AND WHAT ONES WOULD YOU LIKE TO DELETE LIKE AN APP ON YOUR PHONE. THINK ABOUT ONE FOR YOUR NEXT SESSION.

4: HOW WAS YOUR CLIENT RELATIONSHIP TODAY, WHY WAS THIS? WHAT WOULD YOU LIKE TO BE DIFFERENT?

5: WHAT TOOLS HAVE YOU USED TODAY, WHY? DID YOU PREPARE TO USE THEM? IF THIS IS THE CASE WHAT MIGHT YOU HAVE MISSED BY NOT PAYING ATTENTION? WHAT COULD YOU DO DIFFERENTLY NEXT TIME?

6: WHAT WAS YOUR STYLE TODAY? AUTOCRATIC (BOSSY AND AUTHORITIVE) DEMOCRATIC (GUIDE AND PERSONNEL), LAISSEZ-FAIRE (MINDFUL AND RELAXED). REFLECT ON THIS AND WATCH HOW YOU CHANGE, WHAT TRIGGERS YOUR STYLE?

7: HOW MUCH ACTIVE LISTENING DID YOU DO? DID YOU LISTEN TO UNDERSTAND OR LISTEN TO REPLY? A KEY ERROR IS A COACH FORMULATING THE NEXT QUESTION INSTEAD OF LISTENING.

8: IF YOU USED NO TOOLS OR TECHNIQUES TODAY HOW DID THAT MAKE YOU FEEL? DID YOU LEAVE THINKING YOU MISSED SOMETHING? WHAT COULD YOU CHANGE FOR NEXT TIME?

9: WHAT PERCENTAGE OF THE SESSION WAS DRIVEN BY YOU? HOW MUCH OF THE SESSION WERE YOU RELAXED AND NOTICED WHAT CAME UP IN THE SESSION?

10: HOW MUCH OF THE SESSION WAS ABOUT YOU AND HOW MUCH ABOUT THE CLIENT? HOW COULD YOU LOOK AT THIS IN MORE DETAIL?

DATE:-   /   /

1: HOW MUCH GUIDING VS TELLING DID YOU DO? WHO WAS THIS FOR YOU OR THE CLIENT? WHAT COULD YOU DO DIFFERENTLY TO GROW?

2: WHAT MODELS HAVE YOU USED TODAY? BEHAVIOURAL MODELS OR NOTICING EMOTIONS AND FEELINGS? WHAT COULD YOU THINK ABOUT DIFFERENTLY FOR THE NEXT SESSION?

3: HOW MUCH OF YOUR WORK IS A HABIT? WHAT NEW HABITS WOULD YOU LIKE TO CREATE AND WHAT ONES WOULD YOU LIKE TO DELETE LIKE AN APP ON YOUR PHONE. THINK ABOUT ONE FOR YOUR NEXT SESSION.

4: HOW WAS YOUR CLIENT RELATIONSHIP TODAY, WHY WAS THIS? WHAT WOULD YOU LIKE TO BE DIFFERENT?

5: WHAT TOOLS HAVE YOU USED TODAY, WHY? DID YOU PREPARE TO USE THEM? IF THIS IS THE CASE WHAT MIGHT YOU HAVE MISSED BY NOT PAYING ATTENTION? WHAT COULD YOU DO DIFFERENTLY NEXT TIME?

6: WHAT WAS YOUR STYLE TODAY? AUTOCRATIC (BOSSY AND AUTHORITIVE) DEMOCRATIC (GUIDE AND PERSONNEL), LAISSEZ-FAIRE (MINDFUL AND RELAXED). REFLECT ON THIS AND WATCH HOW YOU CHANGE, WHAT TRIGGERS YOUR STYLE?

7: HOW MUCH ACTIVE LISTENING DID YOU DO? DID YOU LISTEN TO UNDERSTAND OR LISTEN TO REPLY? A KEY ERROR IS A COACH FORMULATING THE NEXT QUESTION INSTEAD OF LISTENING.

8: IF YOU USED NO TOOLS OR TECHNIQUES TODAY HOW DID THAT MAKE YOU FEEL? DID YOU LEAVE THINKING YOU MISSED SOMETHING? WHAT COULD YOU CHANGE FOR NEXT TIME?

9: WHAT PERCENTAGE OF THE SESSION WAS DRIVEN BY YOU? HOW MUCH OF THE SESSION WERE YOU RELAXED AND NOTICED WHAT CAME UP IN THE SESSION?

10: HOW MUCH OF THE SESSION WAS ABOUT YOU AND HOW MUCH ABOUT THE CLIENT? HOW COULD YOU LOOK AT THIS IN MORE DETAIL?

DATE:- / /

1: HOW MUCH GUIDING VS TELLING DID YOU DO? WHO WAS THIS FOR YOU OR THE CLIENT? WHAT COULD YOU DO DIFFERENTLY TO GROW?

2: WHAT MODELS HAVE YOU USED TODAY? BEHAVIOURAL MODELS OR NOTICING EMOTIONS AND FEELINGS? WHAT COULD YOU THINK ABOUT DIFFERENTLY FOR THE NEXT SESSION?

3: HOW MUCH OF YOUR WORK IS A HABIT? WHAT NEW HABITS WOULD YOU LIKE TO CREATE AND WHAT ONES WOULD YOU LIKE TO DELETE LIKE AN APP ON YOUR PHONE. THINK ABOUT ONE FOR YOUR NEXT SESSION.

4: HOW WAS YOUR CLIENT RELATIONSHIP TODAY, WHY WAS THIS? WHAT WOULD YOU LIKE TO BE DIFFERENT?

5: WHAT TOOLS HAVE YOU USED TODAY, WHY? DID YOU PREPARE TO USE THEM? IF THIS IS THE CASE WHAT MIGHT YOU HAVE MISSED BY NOT PAYING ATTENTION? WHAT COULD YOU DO DIFFERENTLY NEXT TIME?

6: WHAT WAS YOUR STYLE TODAY? AUTOCRATIC (BOSSY AND AUTHORITIVE) DEMOCRATIC (GUIDE AND PERSONNEL), LAISSEZ-FAIRE (MINDFUL AND RELAXED). REFLECT ON THIS AND WATCH HOW YOU CHANGE, WHAT TRIGGERS YOUR STYLE?

7: HOW MUCH ACTIVE LISTENING DID YOU DO? DID YOU LISTEN TO UNDERSTAND OR LISTEN TO REPLY? A KEY ERROR IS A COACH FORMULATING THE NEXT QUESTION INSTEAD OF LISTENING.

8: IF YOU USED NO TOOLS OR TECHNIQUES TODAY HOW DID THAT MAKE YOU FEEL? DID YOU LEAVE THINKING YOU MISSED SOMETHING? WHAT COULD YOU CHANGE FOR NEXT TIME?

9: WHAT PERCENTAGE OF THE SESSION WAS DRIVEN BY YOU? HOW MUCH OF THE SESSION WERE YOU RELAXED AND NOTICED WHAT CAME UP IN THE SESSION?

10: HOW MUCH OF THE SESSION WAS ABOUT YOU AND HOW MUCH ABOUT THE CLIENT? HOW COULD YOU LOOK AT THIS IN MORE DETAIL?

REFLECTION ON YOUR USE OF TOOLS AND TECHNIQUES IN COACHING

DATE:-   /   /

1: HOW MUCH GUIDING VS TELLING DID YOU DO? WHO WAS THIS FOR YOU OR THE CLIENT? WHAT COULD YOU DO DIFFERENTLY TO GROW?

2: WHAT MODELS HAVE YOU USED TODAY? BEHAVIOURAL MODELS OR NOTICING EMOTIONS AND FEELINGS? WHAT COULD YOU THINK ABOUT DIFFERENTLY FOR THE NEXT SESSION?

3: HOW MUCH OF YOUR WORK IS A HABIT? WHAT NEW HABITS WOULD YOU LIKE TO CREATE AND WHAT ONES WOULD YOU LIKE TO DELETE LIKE AN APP ON YOUR PHONE. THINK ABOUT ONE FOR YOUR NEXT SESSION.

4: HOW WAS YOUR CLIENT RELATIONSHIP TODAY, WHY WAS THIS? WHAT WOULD YOU LIKE TO BE DIFFERENT?

5: WHAT TOOLS HAVE YOU USED TODAY, WHY? DID YOU PREPARE TO USE THEM? IF THIS IS THE CASE WHAT MIGHT YOU HAVE MISSED BY NOT PAYING ATTENTION? WHAT COULD YOU DO DIFFERENTLY NEXT TIME?

6: WHAT WAS YOUR STYLE TODAY? AUTOCRATIC (BOSSY AND AUTHORITIVE) DEMOCRATIC (GUIDE AND PERSONNEL), LAISSEZ-FAIRE (MINDFUL AND RELAXED). REFLECT ON THIS AND WATCH HOW YOU CHANGE, WHAT TRIGGERS YOUR STYLE?

7: HOW MUCH ACTIVE LISTENING DID YOU DO? DID YOU LISTEN TO UNDERSTAND OR LISTEN TO REPLY? A KEY ERROR IS A COACH FORMULATING THE NEXT QUESTION INSTEAD OF LISTENING.

8: IF YOU USED NO TOOLS OR TECHNIQUES TODAY HOW DID THAT MAKE YOU FEEL? DID YOU LEAVE THINKING YOU MISSED SOMETHING? WHAT COULD YOU CHANGE FOR NEXT TIME?

9: WHAT PERCENTAGE OF THE SESSION WAS DRIVEN BY YOU? HOW MUCH OF THE SESSION WERE YOU RELAXED AND NOTICED WHAT CAME UP IN THE SESSION?

10: HOW MUCH OF THE SESSION WAS ABOUT YOU AND HOW MUCH ABOUT THE CLIENT? HOW COULD YOU LOOK AT THIS IN MORE DETAIL?

DATE:-   /   /

1: HOW MUCH GUIDING VS TELLING DID YOU DO? WHO WAS THIS FOR YOU OR THE CLIENT? WHAT COULD YOU DO DIFFERENTLY TO GROW?

2: WHAT MODELS HAVE YOU USED TODAY? BEHAVIOURAL MODELS OR NOTICING EMOTIONS AND FEELINGS? WHAT COULD YOU THINK ABOUT DIFFERENTLY FOR THE NEXT SESSION?

3: HOW MUCH OF YOUR WORK IS A HABIT? WHAT NEW HABITS WOULD YOU LIKE TO CREATE AND WHAT ONES WOULD YOU LIKE TO DELETE LIKE AN APP ON YOUR PHONE. THINK ABOUT ONE FOR YOUR NEXT SESSION.

4: HOW WAS YOUR CLIENT RELATIONSHIP TODAY, WHY WAS THIS? WHAT WOULD YOU LIKE TO BE DIFFERENT?

5: WHAT TOOLS HAVE YOU USED TODAY, WHY? DID YOU PREPARE TO USE THEM? IF THIS IS THE CASE WHAT MIGHT YOU HAVE MISSED BY NOT PAYING ATTENTION? WHAT COULD YOU DO DIFFERENTLY NEXT TIME?

6: WHAT WAS YOUR STYLE TODAY? AUTOCRATIC (BOSSY AND AUTHORITIVE) DEMOCRATIC (GUIDE AND PERSONNEL), LAISSEZ-FAIRE (MINDFUL AND RELAXED). REFLECT ON THIS AND WATCH HOW YOU CHANGE, WHAT TRIGGERS YOUR STYLE?

7: HOW MUCH ACTIVE LISTENING DID YOU DO? DID YOU LISTEN TO UNDERSTAND OR LISTEN TO REPLY? A KEY ERROR IS A COACH FORMULATING THE NEXT QUESTION INSTEAD OF LISTENING.

8: IF YOU USED NO TOOLS OR TECHNIQUES TODAY HOW DID THAT MAKE YOU FEEL? DID YOU LEAVE THINKING YOU MISSED SOMETHING? WHAT COULD YOU CHANGE FOR NEXT TIME?

9: WHAT PERCENTAGE OF THE SESSION WAS DRIVEN BY YOU? HOW MUCH OF THE SESSION WERE YOU RELAXED AND NOTICED WHAT CAME UP IN THE SESSION?

10: HOW MUCH OF THE SESSION WAS ABOUT YOU AND HOW MUCH ABOUT THE CLIENT? HOW COULD YOU LOOK AT THIS IN MORE DETAIL?

DATE:-   /   /

1: HOW MUCH GUIDING VS TELLING DID YOU DO? WHO WAS THIS FOR YOU OR THE CLIENT? WHAT COULD YOU DO DIFFERENTLY TO GROW?

2: WHAT MODELS HAVE YOU USED TODAY? BEHAVIOURAL MODELS OR NOTICING EMOTIONS AND FEELINGS? WHAT COULD YOU THINK ABOUT DIFFERENTLY FOR THE NEXT SESSION?

3: HOW MUCH OF YOUR WORK IS A HABIT? WHAT NEW HABITS WOULD YOU LIKE TO CREATE AND WHAT ONES WOULD YOU LIKE TO DELETE LIKE AN APP ON YOUR PHONE. THINK ABOUT ONE FOR YOUR NEXT SESSION.

4: HOW WAS YOUR CLIENT RELATIONSHIP TODAY, WHY WAS THIS? WHAT WOULD YOU LIKE TO BE DIFFERENT?

5: WHAT TOOLS HAVE YOU USED TODAY, WHY? DID YOU PREPARE TO USE THEM? IF THIS IS THE CASE WHAT MIGHT YOU HAVE MISSED BY NOT PAYING ATTENTION? WHAT COULD YOU DO DIFFERENTLY NEXT TIME?

6: WHAT WAS YOUR STYLE TODAY? AUTOCRATIC (BOSSY AND AUTHORITIVE) DEMOCRATIC (GUIDE AND PERSONNEL), LAISSEZ-FAIRE (MINDFUL AND RELAXED). REFLECT ON THIS AND WATCH HOW YOU CHANGE, WHAT TRIGGERS YOUR STYLE?

7: HOW MUCH ACTIVE LISTENING DID YOU DO? DID YOU LISTEN TO UNDERSTAND OR LISTEN TO REPLY? A KEY ERROR IS A COACH FORMULATING THE NEXT QUESTION INSTEAD OF LISTENING.

8: IF YOU USED NO TOOLS OR TECHNIQUES TODAY HOW DID THAT MAKE YOU FEEL? DID YOU LEAVE THINKING YOU MISSED SOMETHING? WHAT COULD YOU CHANGE FOR NEXT TIME?

9: WHAT PERCENTAGE OF THE SESSION WAS DRIVEN BY YOU? HOW MUCH OF THE SESSION WERE YOU RELAXED AND NOTICED WHAT CAME UP IN THE SESSION?

10: HOW MUCH OF THE SESSION WAS ABOUT YOU AND HOW MUCH ABOUT THE CLIENT? HOW COULD YOU LOOK AT THIS IN MORE DETAIL?

DATE:-   /   /

1: HOW MUCH GUIDING VS TELLING DID YOU DO? WHO WAS THIS
FOR YOU OR THE CLIENT? WHAT COULD YOU DO DIFFERENTLY TO GROW?

2: WHAT MODELS HAVE YOU USED TODAY? BEHAVIOURAL MODELS OR
NOTICING EMOTIONS AND FEELINGS? WHAT COULD YOU THINK ABOUT
DIFFERENTLY FOR THE NEXT SESSION?

3: HOW MUCH OF YOUR WORK IS A HABIT? WHAT NEW HABITS WOULD
YOU LIKE TO CREATE AND WHAT ONES WOULD YOU LIKE TO DELETE LIKE
AN APP ON YOUR PHONE. THINK ABOUT ONE FOR YOUR NEXT SESSION.

4: HOW WAS YOUR CLIENT RELATIONSHIP TODAY, WHY WAS THIS?
WHAT WOULD YOU LIKE TO BE DIFFERENT?

5: WHAT TOOLS HAVE YOU USED TODAY, WHY? DID YOU PREPARE TO
USE THEM? IF THIS IS THE CASE WHAT MIGHT YOU HAVE MISSED BY NOT
PAYING ATTENTION? WHAT COULD YOU DO DIFFERENTLY NEXT TIME?

6: WHAT WAS YOUR STYLE TODAY? AUTOCRATIC (BOSSY AND AUTHORITIVE) DEMOCRATIC (GUIDE AND PERSONNEL), LAISSEZ-FAIRE (MINDFUL AND RELAXED). REFLECT ON THIS AND WATCH HOW YOU CHANGE, WHAT TRIGGERS YOUR STYLE?

7: HOW MUCH ACTIVE LISTENING DID YOU DO? DID YOU LISTEN TO UNDERSTAND OR LISTEN TO REPLY? A KEY ERROR IS A COACH FORMULATING THE NEXT QUESTION INSTEAD OF LISTENING.

8: IF YOU USED NO TOOLS OR TECHNIQUES TODAY HOW DID THAT MAKE YOU FEEL? DID YOU LEAVE THINKING YOU MISSED SOMETHING? WHAT COULD YOU CHANGE FOR NEXT TIME?

9: WHAT PERCENTAGE OF THE SESSION WAS DRIVEN BY YOU? HOW MUCH OF THE SESSION WERE YOU RELAXED AND NOTICED WHAT CAME UP IN THE SESSION?

10: HOW MUCH OF THE SESSION WAS ABOUT YOU AND HOW MUCH ABOUT THE CLIENT? HOW COULD YOU LOOK AT THIS IN MORE DETAIL?

DATE:-   /   /

1: HOW MUCH GUIDING VS TELLING DID YOU DO? WHO WAS THIS FOR YOU OR THE CLIENT? WHAT COULD YOU DO DIFFERENTLY TO GROW?

2: WHAT MODELS HAVE YOU USED TODAY? BEHAVIOURAL MODELS OR NOTICING EMOTIONS AND FEELINGS? WHAT COULD YOU THINK ABOUT DIFFERENTLY FOR THE NEXT SESSION?

3: HOW MUCH OF YOUR WORK IS A HABIT? WHAT NEW HABITS WOULD YOU LIKE TO CREATE AND WHAT ONES WOULD YOU LIKE TO DELETE LIKE AN APP ON YOUR PHONE. THINK ABOUT ONE FOR YOUR NEXT SESSION.

4: HOW WAS YOUR CLIENT RELATIONSHIP TODAY, WHY WAS THIS? WHAT WOULD YOU LIKE TO BE DIFFERENT?

5: WHAT TOOLS HAVE YOU USED TODAY, WHY? DID YOU PREPARE TO USE THEM? IF THIS IS THE CASE WHAT MIGHT YOU HAVE MISSED BY NOT PAYING ATTENTION? WHAT COULD YOU DO DIFFERENTLY NEXT TIME?

6: WHAT WAS YOUR STYLE TODAY? AUTOCRATIC (BOSSY AND AUTHORITIVE) DEMOCRATIC (GUIDE AND PERSONNEL), LAISSEZ-FAIRE (MINDFUL AND RELAXED). REFLECT ON THIS AND WATCH HOW YOU CHANGE, WHAT TRIGGERS YOUR STYLE?

7: HOW MUCH ACTIVE LISTENING DID YOU DO? DID YOU LISTEN TO UNDERSTAND OR LISTEN TO REPLY? A KEY ERROR IS A COACH FORMULATING THE NEXT QUESTION INSTEAD OF LISTENING.

8: IF YOU USED NO TOOLS OR TECHNIQUES TODAY HOW DID THAT MAKE YOU FEEL? DID YOU LEAVE THINKING YOU MISSED SOMETHING? WHAT COULD YOU CHANGE FOR NEXT TIME?

9: WHAT PERCENTAGE OF THE SESSION WAS DRIVEN BY YOU? HOW MUCH OF THE SESSION WERE YOU RELAXED AND NOTICED WHAT CAME UP IN THE SESSION?

10: HOW MUCH OF THE SESSION WAS ABOUT YOU AND HOW MUCH ABOUT THE CLIENT? HOW COULD YOU LOOK AT THIS IN MORE DETAIL?

1: HOW HAVE I GROWN OVER THE LAST 10 DAYS

2: WHAT AM I GOING TO FOCUS ON OVER THE NEXT 10 DAYS?

3: WHAT FIVE THINGS AM I POSITIVELY TAKING FROM THE LAST 10 DAYS AND MOVING THEM FORWARD INTO THE NEXT 10 DAYS.

-
-
-
-
-

4: WHAT KEY AREAS WOULD I LIKE TO CONCENTRATE ON?

"There is nothing so uncertain as a sure thing."

SCOTTY BOWMAN

DATE:-   /   /

1: HOW MUCH GUIDING VS TELLING DID YOU DO? WHO WAS THIS FOR YOU OR THE CLIENT? WHAT COULD YOU DO DIFFERENTLY TO GROW?

2: WHAT MODELS HAVE YOU USED TODAY? BEHAVIOURAL MODELS OR NOTICING EMOTIONS AND FEELINGS? WHAT COULD YOU THINK ABOUT DIFFERENTLY FOR THE NEXT SESSION?

3: HOW MUCH OF YOUR WORK IS A HABIT? WHAT NEW HABITS WOULD YOU LIKE TO CREATE AND WHAT ONES WOULD YOU LIKE TO DELETE LIKE AN APP ON YOUR PHONE. THINK ABOUT ONE FOR YOUR NEXT SESSION.

4: HOW WAS YOUR CLIENT RELATIONSHIP TODAY, WHY WAS THIS? WHAT WOULD YOU LIKE TO BE DIFFERENT?

5: WHAT TOOLS HAVE YOU USED TODAY, WHY? DID YOU PREPARE TO USE THEM? IF THIS IS THE CASE WHAT MIGHT YOU HAVE MISSED BY NOT PAYING ATTENTION? WHAT COULD YOU DO DIFFERENTLY NEXT TIME?

6: WHAT WAS YOUR STYLE TODAY? AUTOCRATIC (BOSSY AND AUTHORITIVE) DEMOCRATIC (GUIDE AND PERSONNEL), LAISSEZ-FAIRE (MINDFUL AND RELAXED). REFLECT ON THIS AND WATCH HOW YOU CHANGE, WHAT TRIGGERS YOUR STYLE?

7: HOW MUCH ACTIVE LISTENING DID YOU DO? DID YOU LISTEN TO UNDERSTAND OR LISTEN TO REPLY? A KEY ERROR IS A COACH FORMULATING THE NEXT QUESTION INSTEAD OF LISTENING.

8: IF YOU USED NO TOOLS OR TECHNIQUES TODAY HOW DID THAT MAKE YOU FEEL? DID YOU LEAVE THINKING YOU MISSED SOMETHING? WHAT COULD YOU CHANGE FOR NEXT TIME?

9: WHAT PERCENTAGE OF THE SESSION WAS DRIVEN BY YOU? HOW MUCH OF THE SESSION WERE YOU RELAXED AND NOTICED WHAT CAME UP IN THE SESSION?

10: HOW MUCH OF THE SESSION WAS ABOUT YOU AND HOW MUCH ABOUT THE CLIENT? HOW COULD YOU LOOK AT THIS IN MORE DETAIL?

DATE:-   /   /

1: HOW MUCH GUIDING VS TELLING DID YOU DO? WHO WAS THIS FOR YOU OR THE CLIENT? WHAT COULD YOU DO DIFFERENTLY TO GROW?

2: WHAT MODELS HAVE YOU USED TODAY? BEHAVIOURAL MODELS OR NOTICING EMOTIONS AND FEELINGS? WHAT COULD YOU THINK ABOUT DIFFERENTLY FOR THE NEXT SESSION?

3: HOW MUCH OF YOUR WORK IS A HABIT? WHAT NEW HABITS WOULD YOU LIKE TO CREATE AND WHAT ONES WOULD YOU LIKE TO DELETE LIKE AN APP ON YOUR PHONE. THINK ABOUT ONE FOR YOUR NEXT SESSION.

4: HOW WAS YOUR CLIENT RELATIONSHIP TODAY, WHY WAS THIS? WHAT WOULD YOU LIKE TO BE DIFFERENT?

5: WHAT TOOLS HAVE YOU USED TODAY, WHY? DID YOU PREPARE TO USE THEM? IF THIS IS THE CASE WHAT MIGHT YOU HAVE MISSED BY NOT PAYING ATTENTION? WHAT COULD YOU DO DIFFERENTLY NEXT TIME?

6: WHAT WAS YOUR STYLE TODAY? AUTOCRATIC (BOSSY AND AUTHORITIVE) DEMOCRATIC (GUIDE AND PERSONNEL), LAISSEZ-FAIRE (MINDFUL AND RELAXED). REFLECT ON THIS AND WATCH HOW YOU CHANGE, WHAT TRIGGERS YOUR STYLE?

7: HOW MUCH ACTIVE LISTENING DID YOU DO? DID YOU LISTEN TO UNDERSTAND OR LISTEN TO REPLY? A KEY ERROR IS A COACH FORMULATING THE NEXT QUESTION INSTEAD OF LISTENING.

8: IF YOU USED NO TOOLS OR TECHNIQUES TODAY HOW DID THAT MAKE YOU FEEL? DID YOU LEAVE THINKING YOU MISSED SOMETHING? WHAT COULD YOU CHANGE FOR NEXT TIME?

9: WHAT PERCENTAGE OF THE SESSION WAS DRIVEN BY YOU? HOW MUCH OF THE SESSION WERE YOU RELAXED AND NOTICED WHAT CAME UP IN THE SESSION?

10: HOW MUCH OF THE SESSION WAS ABOUT YOU AND HOW MUCH ABOUT THE CLIENT? HOW COULD YOU LOOK AT THIS IN MORE DETAIL?

DATE:-   /   /

1: HOW MUCH GUIDING VS TELLING DID YOU DO? WHO WAS THIS FOR YOU OR THE CLIENT? WHAT COULD YOU DO DIFFERENTLY TO GROW?

2: WHAT MODELS HAVE YOU USED TODAY? BEHAVIOURAL MODELS OR NOTICING EMOTIONS AND FEELINGS? WHAT COULD YOU THINK ABOUT DIFFERENTLY FOR THE NEXT SESSION?

3: HOW MUCH OF YOUR WORK IS A HABIT? WHAT NEW HABITS WOULD YOU LIKE TO CREATE AND WHAT ONES WOULD YOU LIKE TO DELETE LIKE AN APP ON YOUR PHONE. THINK ABOUT ONE FOR YOUR NEXT SESSION.

4: HOW WAS YOUR CLIENT RELATIONSHIP TODAY, WHY WAS THIS? WHAT WOULD YOU LIKE TO BE DIFFERENT?

5: WHAT TOOLS HAVE YOU USED TODAY, WHY? DID YOU PREPARE TO USE THEM? IF THIS IS THE CASE WHAT MIGHT YOU HAVE MISSED BY NOT PAYING ATTENTION? WHAT COULD YOU DO DIFFERENTLY NEXT TIME?

6: WHAT WAS YOUR STYLE TODAY? AUTOCRATIC (BOSSY AND AUTHORITIVE) DEMOCRATIC (GUIDE AND PERSONNEL), LAISSEZ-FAIRE (MINDFUL AND RELAXED). REFLECT ON THIS AND WATCH HOW YOU CHANGE, WHAT TRIGGERS YOUR STYLE?

7: HOW MUCH ACTIVE LISTENING DID YOU DO? DID YOU LISTEN TO UNDERSTAND OR LISTEN TO REPLY? A KEY ERROR IS A COACH FORMULATING THE NEXT QUESTION INSTEAD OF LISTENING.

8: IF YOU USED NO TOOLS OR TECHNIQUES TODAY HOW DID THAT MAKE YOU FEEL? DID YOU LEAVE THINKING YOU MISSED SOMETHING? WHAT COULD YOU CHANGE FOR NEXT TIME?

9: WHAT PERCENTAGE OF THE SESSION WAS DRIVEN BY YOU? HOW MUCH OF THE SESSION WERE YOU RELAXED AND NOTICED WHAT CAME UP IN THE SESSION?

10: HOW MUCH OF THE SESSION WAS ABOUT YOU AND HOW MUCH ABOUT THE CLIENT? HOW COULD YOU LOOK AT THIS IN MORE DETAIL?

DATE:-   /   /

1: HOW MUCH GUIDING VS TELLING DID YOU DO? WHO WAS THIS FOR YOU OR THE CLIENT? WHAT COULD YOU DO DIFFERENTLY TO GROW?

2: WHAT MODELS HAVE YOU USED TODAY? BEHAVIOURAL MODELS OR NOTICING EMOTIONS AND FEELINGS? WHAT COULD YOU THINK ABOUT DIFFERENTLY FOR THE NEXT SESSION?

3: HOW MUCH OF YOUR WORK IS A HABIT? WHAT NEW HABITS WOULD YOU LIKE TO CREATE AND WHAT ONES WOULD YOU LIKE TO DELETE LIKE AN APP ON YOUR PHONE. THINK ABOUT ONE FOR YOUR NEXT SESSION.

4: HOW WAS YOUR CLIENT RELATIONSHIP TODAY, WHY WAS THIS? WHAT WOULD YOU LIKE TO BE DIFFERENT?

5: WHAT TOOLS HAVE YOU USED TODAY, WHY? DID YOU PREPARE TO USE THEM? IF THIS IS THE CASE WHAT MIGHT YOU HAVE MISSED BY NOT PAYING ATTENTION? WHAT COULD YOU DO DIFFERENTLY NEXT TIME?

6: WHAT WAS YOUR STYLE TODAY? AUTOCRATIC (BOSSY AND AUTHORITIVE) DEMOCRATIC (GUIDE AND PERSONNEL), LAISSEZ-FAIRE (MINDFUL AND RELAXED). REFLECT ON THIS AND WATCH HOW YOU CHANGE, WHAT TRIGGERS YOUR STYLE?

7: HOW MUCH ACTIVE LISTENING DID YOU DO? DID YOU LISTEN TO UNDERSTAND OR LISTEN TO REPLY? A KEY ERROR IS A COACH FORMULATING THE NEXT QUESTION INSTEAD OF LISTENING.

8: IF YOU USED NO TOOLS OR TECHNIQUES TODAY HOW DID THAT MAKE YOU FEEL? DID YOU LEAVE THINKING YOU MISSED SOMETHING? WHAT COULD YOU CHANGE FOR NEXT TIME?

9: WHAT PERCENTAGE OF THE SESSION WAS DRIVEN BY YOU? HOW MUCH OF THE SESSION WERE YOU RELAXED AND NOTICED WHAT CAME UP IN THE SESSION?

10: HOW MUCH OF THE SESSION WAS ABOUT YOU AND HOW MUCH ABOUT THE CLIENT? HOW COULD YOU LOOK AT THIS IN MORE DETAIL?

DATE:-   /   /

1: HOW MUCH GUIDING VS TELLING DID YOU DO? WHO WAS THIS
FOR YOU OR THE CLIENT? WHAT COULD YOU DO DIFFERENTLY TO GROW?

2: WHAT MODELS HAVE YOU USED TODAY? BEHAVIOURAL MODELS OR
NOTICING EMOTIONS AND FEELINGS? WHAT COULD YOU THINK ABOUT
DIFFERENTLY FOR THE NEXT SESSION?

3: HOW MUCH OF YOUR WORK IS A HABIT? WHAT NEW HABITS WOULD
YOU LIKE TO CREATE AND WHAT ONES WOULD YOU LIKE TO DELETE LIKE
AN APP ON YOUR PHONE. THINK ABOUT ONE FOR YOUR NEXT SESSION.

4: HOW WAS YOUR CLIENT RELATIONSHIP TODAY, WHY WAS THIS?
WHAT WOULD YOU LIKE TO BE DIFFERENT?

5: WHAT TOOLS HAVE YOU USED TODAY, WHY? DID YOU PREPARE TO
USE THEM? IF THIS IS THE CASE WHAT MIGHT YOU HAVE MISSED BY NOT
PAYING ATTENTION? WHAT COULD YOU DO DIFFERENTLY NEXT TIME?

6: WHAT WAS YOUR STYLE TODAY? AUTOCRATIC (BOSSY AND AUTHORITIVE) DEMOCRATIC (GUIDE AND PERSONNEL), LAISSEZ-FAIRE (MINDFUL AND RELAXED). REFLECT ON THIS AND WATCH HOW YOU CHANGE, WHAT TRIGGERS YOUR STYLE?

7: HOW MUCH ACTIVE LISTENING DID YOU DO? DID YOU LISTEN TO UNDERSTAND OR LISTEN TO REPLY? A KEY ERROR IS A COACH FORMULATING THE NEXT QUESTION INSTEAD OF LISTENING.

8: IF YOU USED NO TOOLS OR TECHNIQUES TODAY HOW DID THAT MAKE YOU FEEL? DID YOU LEAVE THINKING YOU MISSED SOMETHING? WHAT COULD YOU CHANGE FOR NEXT TIME?

9: WHAT PERCENTAGE OF THE SESSION WAS DRIVEN BY YOU? HOW MUCH OF THE SESSION WERE YOU RELAXED AND NOTICED WHAT CAME UP IN THE SESSION?

10: HOW MUCH OF THE SESSION WAS ABOUT YOU AND HOW MUCH ABOUT THE CLIENT? HOW COULD YOU LOOK AT THIS IN MORE DETAIL?

DATE:-   /   /

1: HOW MUCH GUIDING VS TELLING DID YOU DO? WHO WAS THIS FOR YOU OR THE CLIENT? WHAT COULD YOU DO DIFFERENTLY TO GROW?

2: WHAT MODELS HAVE YOU USED TODAY? BEHAVIOURAL MODELS OR NOTICING EMOTIONS AND FEELINGS? WHAT COULD YOU THINK ABOUT DIFFERENTLY FOR THE NEXT SESSION?

3: HOW MUCH OF YOUR WORK IS A HABIT? WHAT NEW HABITS WOULD YOU LIKE TO CREATE AND WHAT ONES WOULD YOU LIKE TO DELETE LIKE AN APP ON YOUR PHONE. THINK ABOUT ONE FOR YOUR NEXT SESSION.

4: HOW WAS YOUR CLIENT RELATIONSHIP TODAY, WHY WAS THIS? WHAT WOULD YOU LIKE TO BE DIFFERENT?

5: WHAT TOOLS HAVE YOU USED TODAY, WHY? DID YOU PREPARE TO USE THEM? IF THIS IS THE CASE WHAT MIGHT YOU HAVE MISSED BY NOT PAYING ATTENTION? WHAT COULD YOU DO DIFFERENTLY NEXT TIME?

6: WHAT WAS YOUR STYLE TODAY? AUTOCRATIC (BOSSY AND AUTHORITIVE) DEMOCRATIC (GUIDE AND PERSONNEL), LAISSEZ-FAIRE (MINDFUL AND RELAXED). REFLECT ON THIS AND WATCH HOW YOU CHANGE, WHAT TRIGGERS YOUR STYLE?

7: HOW MUCH ACTIVE LISTENING DID YOU DO? DID YOU LISTEN TO UNDERSTAND OR LISTEN TO REPLY? A KEY ERROR IS A COACH FORMULATING THE NEXT QUESTION INSTEAD OF LISTENING.

8: IF YOU USED NO TOOLS OR TECHNIQUES TODAY HOW DID THAT MAKE YOU FEEL? DID YOU LEAVE THINKING YOU MISSED SOMETHING? WHAT COULD YOU CHANGE FOR NEXT TIME?

9: WHAT PERCENTAGE OF THE SESSION WAS DRIVEN BY YOU? HOW MUCH OF THE SESSION WERE YOU RELAXED AND NOTICED WHAT CAME UP IN THE SESSION?

10: HOW MUCH OF THE SESSION WAS ABOUT YOU AND HOW MUCH ABOUT THE CLIENT? HOW COULD YOU LOOK AT THIS IN MORE DETAIL?

DATE:-   /   /

1: HOW MUCH GUIDING VS TELLING DID YOU DO? WHO WAS THIS FOR YOU OR THE CLIENT? WHAT COULD YOU DO DIFFERENTLY TO GROW?

2: WHAT MODELS HAVE YOU USED TODAY? BEHAVIOURAL MODELS OR NOTICING EMOTIONS AND FEELINGS? WHAT COULD YOU THINK ABOUT DIFFERENTLY FOR THE NEXT SESSION?

3: HOW MUCH OF YOUR WORK IS A HABIT? WHAT NEW HABITS WOULD YOU LIKE TO CREATE AND WHAT ONES WOULD YOU LIKE TO DELETE LIKE AN APP ON YOUR PHONE. THINK ABOUT ONE FOR YOUR NEXT SESSION.

4: HOW WAS YOUR CLIENT RELATIONSHIP TODAY, WHY WAS THIS? WHAT WOULD YOU LIKE TO BE DIFFERENT?

5: WHAT TOOLS HAVE YOU USED TODAY, WHY? DID YOU PREPARE TO USE THEM? IF THIS IS THE CASE WHAT MIGHT YOU HAVE MISSED BY NOT PAYING ATTENTION? WHAT COULD YOU DO DIFFERENTLY NEXT TIME?

6: WHAT WAS YOUR STYLE TODAY? AUTOCRATIC (BOSSY AND AUTHORITIVE) DEMOCRATIC (GUIDE AND PERSONNEL), LAISSEZ-FAIRE (MINDFUL AND RELAXED). REFLECT ON THIS AND WATCH HOW YOU CHANGE, WHAT TRIGGERS YOUR STYLE?

7: HOW MUCH ACTIVE LISTENING DID YOU DO? DID YOU LISTEN TO UNDERSTAND OR LISTEN TO REPLY? A KEY ERROR IS A COACH FORMULATING THE NEXT QUESTION INSTEAD OF LISTENING.

8: IF YOU USED NO TOOLS OR TECHNIQUES TODAY HOW DID THAT MAKE YOU FEEL? DID YOU LEAVE THINKING YOU MISSED SOMETHING? WHAT COULD YOU CHANGE FOR NEXT TIME?

9: WHAT PERCENTAGE OF THE SESSION WAS DRIVEN BY YOU? HOW MUCH OF THE SESSION WERE YOU RELAXED AND NOTICED WHAT CAME UP IN THE SESSION?

10: HOW MUCH OF THE SESSION WAS ABOUT YOU AND HOW MUCH ABOUT THE CLIENT? HOW COULD YOU LOOK AT THIS IN MORE DETAIL?

DATE:-   /   /

1: HOW MUCH GUIDING VS TELLING DID YOU DO? WHO WAS THIS FOR YOU OR THE CLIENT? WHAT COULD YOU DO DIFFERENTLY TO GROW?

2: WHAT MODELS HAVE YOU USED TODAY? BEHAVIOURAL MODELS OR NOTICING EMOTIONS AND FEELINGS? WHAT COULD YOU THINK ABOUT DIFFERENTLY FOR THE NEXT SESSION?

3: HOW MUCH OF YOUR WORK IS A HABIT? WHAT NEW HABITS WOULD YOU LIKE TO CREATE AND WHAT ONES WOULD YOU LIKE TO DELETE LIKE AN APP ON YOUR PHONE. THINK ABOUT ONE FOR YOUR NEXT SESSION.

4: HOW WAS YOUR CLIENT RELATIONSHIP TODAY, WHY WAS THIS? WHAT WOULD YOU LIKE TO BE DIFFERENT?

5: WHAT TOOLS HAVE YOU USED TODAY, WHY? DID YOU PREPARE TO USE THEM? IF THIS IS THE CASE WHAT MIGHT YOU HAVE MISSED BY NOT PAYING ATTENTION? WHAT COULD YOU DO DIFFERENTLY NEXT TIME?

6: WHAT WAS YOUR STYLE TODAY? AUTOCRATIC (BOSSY AND AUTHORITIVE) DEMOCRATIC (GUIDE AND PERSONNEL), LAISSEZ-FAIRE (MINDFUL AND RELAXED). REFLECT ON THIS AND WATCH HOW YOU CHANGE, WHAT TRIGGERS YOUR STYLE?

7: HOW MUCH ACTIVE LISTENING DID YOU DO? DID YOU LISTEN TO UNDERSTAND OR LISTEN TO REPLY? A KEY ERROR IS A COACH FORMULATING THE NEXT QUESTION INSTEAD OF LISTENING.

8: IF YOU USED NO TOOLS OR TECHNIQUES TODAY HOW DID THAT MAKE YOU FEEL? DID YOU LEAVE THINKING YOU MISSED SOMETHING? WHAT COULD YOU CHANGE FOR NEXT TIME?

9: WHAT PERCENTAGE OF THE SESSION WAS DRIVEN BY YOU? HOW MUCH OF THE SESSION WERE YOU RELAXED AND NOTICED WHAT CAME UP IN THE SESSION?

10: HOW MUCH OF THE SESSION WAS ABOUT YOU AND HOW MUCH ABOUT THE CLIENT? HOW COULD YOU LOOK AT THIS IN MORE DETAIL?

DATE:-   /   /

1: HOW MUCH GUIDING VS TELLING DID YOU DO? WHO WAS THIS
FOR YOU OR THE CLIENT? WHAT COULD YOU DO DIFFERENTLY TO GROW?

2: WHAT MODELS HAVE YOU USED TODAY? BEHAVIOURAL MODELS OR
NOTICING EMOTIONS AND FEELINGS? WHAT COULD YOU THINK ABOUT
DIFFERENTLY FOR THE NEXT SESSION?

3: HOW MUCH OF YOUR WORK IS A HABIT? WHAT NEW HABITS WOULD
YOU LIKE TO CREATE AND WHAT ONES WOULD YOU LIKE TO DELETE LIKE
AN APP ON YOUR PHONE. THINK ABOUT ONE FOR YOUR NEXT SESSION.

4: HOW WAS YOUR CLIENT RELATIONSHIP TODAY, WHY WAS THIS?
WHAT WOULD YOU LIKE TO BE DIFFERENT?

5: WHAT TOOLS HAVE YOU USED TODAY, WHY? DID YOU PREPARE TO
USE THEM? IF THIS IS THE CASE WHAT MIGHT YOU HAVE MISSED BY NOT
PAYING ATTENTION? WHAT COULD YOU DO DIFFERENTLY NEXT TIME?

6: WHAT WAS YOUR STYLE TODAY? AUTOCRATIC (BOSSY AND AUTHORITIVE) DEMOCRATIC (GUIDE AND PERSONNEL), LAISSEZ-FAIRE (MINDFUL AND RELAXED). REFLECT ON THIS AND WATCH HOW YOU CHANGE, WHAT TRIGGERS YOUR STYLE?

7: HOW MUCH ACTIVE LISTENING DID YOU DO? DID YOU LISTEN TO UNDERSTAND OR LISTEN TO REPLY? A KEY ERROR IS A COACH FORMULATING THE NEXT QUESTION INSTEAD OF LISTENING.

8: IF YOU USED NO TOOLS OR TECHNIQUES TODAY HOW DID THAT MAKE YOU FEEL? DID YOU LEAVE THINKING YOU MISSED SOMETHING? WHAT COULD YOU CHANGE FOR NEXT TIME?

9: WHAT PERCENTAGE OF THE SESSION WAS DRIVEN BY YOU? HOW MUCH OF THE SESSION WERE YOU RELAXED AND NOTICED WHAT CAME UP IN THE SESSION?

10: HOW MUCH OF THE SESSION WAS ABOUT YOU AND HOW MUCH ABOUT THE CLIENT? HOW COULD YOU LOOK AT THIS IN MORE DETAIL?

DATE:-   /   /

1: HOW MUCH GUIDING VS TELLING DID YOU DO? WHO WAS THIS FOR YOU OR THE CLIENT? WHAT COULD YOU DO DIFFERENTLY TO GROW?

2: WHAT MODELS HAVE YOU USED TODAY? BEHAVIOURAL MODELS OR NOTICING EMOTIONS AND FEELINGS? WHAT COULD YOU THINK ABOUT DIFFERENTLY FOR THE NEXT SESSION?

3: HOW MUCH OF YOUR WORK IS A HABIT? WHAT NEW HABITS WOULD YOU LIKE TO CREATE AND WHAT ONES WOULD YOU LIKE TO DELETE LIKE AN APP ON YOUR PHONE. THINK ABOUT ONE FOR YOUR NEXT SESSION.

4: HOW WAS YOUR CLIENT RELATIONSHIP TODAY, WHY WAS THIS? WHAT WOULD YOU LIKE TO BE DIFFERENT?

5: WHAT TOOLS HAVE YOU USED TODAY, WHY? DID YOU PREPARE TO USE THEM? IF THIS IS THE CASE WHAT MIGHT YOU HAVE MISSED BY NOT PAYING ATTENTION? WHAT COULD YOU DO DIFFERENTLY NEXT TIME?

6: WHAT WAS YOUR STYLE TODAY? AUTOCRATIC (BOSSY AND AUTHORITIVE) DEMOCRATIC (GUIDE AND PERSONNEL), LAISSEZ-FAIRE (MINDFUL AND RELAXED). REFLECT ON THIS AND WATCH HOW YOU CHANGE, WHAT TRIGGERS YOUR STYLE?

7: HOW MUCH ACTIVE LISTENING DID YOU DO? DID YOU LISTEN TO UNDERSTAND OR LISTEN TO REPLY? A KEY ERROR IS A COACH FORMULATING THE NEXT QUESTION INSTEAD OF LISTENING.

8: IF YOU USED NO TOOLS OR TECHNIQUES TODAY HOW DID THAT MAKE YOU FEEL? DID YOU LEAVE THINKING YOU MISSED SOMETHING? WHAT COULD YOU CHANGE FOR NEXT TIME?

9: WHAT PERCENTAGE OF THE SESSION WAS DRIVEN BY YOU? HOW MUCH OF THE SESSION WERE YOU RELAXED AND NOTICED WHAT CAME UP IN THE SESSION?

10: HOW MUCH OF THE SESSION WAS ABOUT YOU AND HOW MUCH ABOUT THE CLIENT? HOW COULD YOU LOOK AT THIS IN MORE DETAIL?

1: HOW HAVE I GROWN OVER THE LAST 10 DAYS

2: WHAT AM I GOING TO FOCUS ON OVER THE NEXT 10 DAYS?

3: WHAT FIVE THINGS AM I POSITIVELY TAKING FROM THE LAST 10 DAYS AND MOVING THEM FORWARD INTO THE NEXT 10 DAYS.

-
-
-
-
-

4: WHAT KEY AREAS WOULD I LIKE TO CONCENTRATE ON?

Day 100
Congratulations

Congratulations on achieving 100 days. You have completed and reflected on use of coaching tools and techniques. You have created some very positive actions. You have our permission to give yourself an award for achieving this fantastic milestone. Now think about how you can take this forward and grow further, amazing stuff.

WHAT HAVE I LEARNT AND HOW AM I GOING TO IMPLEMENT THIS IN THE FUTURE

WRITE FIVE THINGS THAT YOU HAVE BECOME MUCH MORE AWARE OF. THE JOURNAL HAS GIVEN YOU LITTLE SPACES TO WRITE KEY THINGS DOWN, OBVIOUSLY THE GREATER THE REFLECTION THE MORE YOU IMPROVE. THE PROBLEM IS NOT EVERYONE IS AWARE WRITING DOWN WORKS, THIS JOURNAL KEEPS IT EASY FOR YOU.

GOOD LUCK WITH MOVING FORWARD, BE PROUD OF YOURSELF.

1..

2..

3..

4..

5..

If you have enjoyed this journal please leave us a review on Amazon.

NOTES

NOTES

JCRM JOURNALS
MEET THE AUTHORS

RALPH MOODY

Ralph believes that lifelong learning is precisely that, and should not be limited by age or perceived ability. He has a belief that all of us have the potential to do anything if we put our minds to it. Armed with the right skills, knowledge and attitude, we can all perform to the highest standards. Moreover, his philosophy is that limiting belief is what holds the majority of people back and that, with appropriate coaching, mentoring and training, we can all achieve anything. With over 30 years of training experience, he specialises in trainer, management and leadership development.

> *"Life is a gift and we all have a responsibility to make the most of it, so that when we look back, we know it wasn't wasted"*
>
> RALPH MOODY

CLAIRE MOODY

Claire is an extremely experienced trainer and coach at Target Training, and you can always guarantee she will deliver outstanding results: she is incredibly passionate about both her training and coaching. She has over 35 years' experience in training, coaching and quality assurance roles, with experience as a teacher and in Train the Trainer, working with international clients. Moreover, she has expertise in the management of trainer inductions, standardisation and quality assurance for corporate clients. She holds an MSc in executive coaching and is accredited by Ashridge, a world leader in executive coach training and development. Additionally, she specialises in psychometric assessment, including MBTI.

> *"It's not about being the best, it's about being the best you can be"*
>
> CLAIRE MOODY

HAVE QUESTIONS?

Target Training Associates
107 Cheapside, London, EC2V 6DN
0800 302 9344
info@targettrg.co.uk
www.targettrg.co.uk
www.jcrm.shop

SOME OTHER TITLES IN THE JOURNAL SERIES

Coaching Journal
Law of Attraction Journal
Being Positive Journal
Improve Self-Esteem Journal
Do I or don't I deal with conflict Journal
Action Planning Journal
Management Journal
Rainbow Foods Journal

Contact us for a quote for a bespoke journal for your particular organisation

Printed in Great Britain
by Amazon

40519136R00131